DO LESS, BE MORE

DO LESS, BE MORE

A 5-step guide to becoming a Leader of Substance

VANESSA PORTER

'Vanessa's approach to leadership through her five steps is immensely relevant and meaningful for leaders in our current business environment. *Do Less, BE More* is a valuable toolkit for us all to reflect upon and focus on what really matters, our people. We need to empower ourselves so our teams think more, not just do. Vanessa's insights support a framework of purpose for all stakeholders to be highly successful.'

Brett Houldin, Chief Executive Officer, Craveable Brands

For my mum Antoinette, who was resilient, determined and strong, coupled with huge stores of warmth and grace. This one is for you.

ACKNOWLEDGEMENTS

My dad Walter Broadbent was wise, a patient teacher and my first mentor. In his career, he was a true leader in the retail industry across three continents, and later, a psychotherapist/hypnotherapist with his own practice in the famous Harley Street, London. He showed me, at an early age, the power of tapping into your subconscious to achieve extraordinary results. I thank him for being my amazing example.

Special mention to Frank McManus who has been my client, my leader and a dear friend. You are relentless at seeing what is possible. You approach each day with inspirational zest and passion. You provide me with countless opportunities and consistently back me.

Denis Bourke for being my mentor throughout my career in Australia. I am lucky to have learnt from the master by seeing you in action. You take complex theory and distil it into easy-to-digest bite-sized pieces. You give it a practical context, always relating it back to solving business challenges. You have a heck of a lot of fun at the same time.

Adeline Lane who is like a sister to me. Your command of the English language is like no other. Your vocabulary is beyond extensive. You have helped me to use writing as an expression in the toughest of times. Most notably in my parents' eulogies and the last two hundred and fifty-four words of this book.

Ian Flemington who was a colleague, is a client and a best friend. We have partnered in our professional and personal lives and conquered many obstacles to achieve great success. Thank you for your consistent support and bringing the 'Fleia' factor that only you can.

A big thank you to Kemi Nekvapil for your coaching and guidance to make this book a reality.

Kath Walters for saying "keep writing in the cracks". You are right; this really works. It boosted my writing momentum.

To the visionaries who share my belief in the future of Leadership, I thank you. Your courage to step boldly into the unknown and trust me to challenge you is truly appreciated.

From the seasoned professionals to the newbies, without your willingness to try something new, a book like this just wouldn't be possible.

Deep gratitude.

First published in 2018 by Vanessa Porter
www.allofyou.co

A catalogue entry for this book is available from the National Library of Australia.

ISBN: 978-1-925648-72-0

Typeset in 11.5/15.5 pt Berkeley
Project management and text design by Michael Hanrahan Publishing
Cover design by Peter Reardon

Disclaimer
The material in this publication is of the nature of general comment only and does not represent professional advice. It is not intended to provide specific guidance for any particular circumstances and it should not be relied upon for any decision to take action or not to take action on any matter, which it covers. Reader should obtain professional advice where appropriate, before making any such decision. To the maximum extent permitted by law, the author and publisher disclaim all responsibility and liability to any person, arising directly or indirectly from any person taking or not taking action based on the information in this book.

CONTENTS

INTRODUCTION

There comes a time when we need to step up and hold ourselves accountable for creating a thriving environment— for ourselves, our people and for our organisations.

Leaders tell me they feel constantly overwhelmed, out of control and disconnected from their people and their own lives. Their days are sabotaged by urgent emails from daybreak, their structured plans derailed by operational demands and the frequent escalation of internal issues in the ever-increasing reach and speed of the glare of public and media scrutiny. At the business day's end, a glass of wine and mind-numbing television wins out over creative contemplation time.

I am all too familiar with days as a leader under constant bombardment, reacting to the latest crisis. Within a short time, this became a growing frustration for me about being deprived of the chance to implement my carefully conceived strategic plans. My sense of personal achievement and happiness suffered, and my inner critic took hold of my self-confidence. None of this helped my workplace's productivity or success.

The option of escape seemed limited to checking out or walking out. I took the second road. But the reality is that option is not available to everyone. And you and your organisation may suffer with either choice.

Is there another way to tackle the leadership merry-go-round? My research identified the common woes leaders suffer as: working in the business rather than on it, not being as genuinely connected to people as needed to inspire discretionary effort and lacking a clear sense of what matters most.

Leaders of Substance are those who manage the demands of their role differently. They focus less on 'doing' and more on 'being', with transformational results.

The aim of this book is to make Leaders of Substance of those who are currently lost in the operational grind of the business, who feel the lack of robust relationships and who are ambushed by relentless disruptions. If that is you, take heart. This book is for you.

Thoughts and feelings are temporary; they come and go. However, sometimes they stick around for much longer than is helpful. Becoming aware of our thoughts and emotions, noticing them, recognising them and being mindful of them means we can make choices about them. By being an observer of our thoughts and emotions, we immediately create distance from them and gain perspective: 'Oh look, I can feel myself getting tense and feeling irritated because she is using my special cup again'.

This skill of noticing requires you to be present, engaged and focused on what is going on right now, rather than being distracted about things that are going to happen later. In many cases, people are busy making mental lists of everything to be done later today or reviewing what happened in the past.

Being present is the key to managing your emotions and managing your stress levels. You feel calmer when you are just dealing with the present moment.

Regardless of what county, industry or sector, organisations are full of people whom respond to the five-step methodology I describe in this book. Many people have had great success from adopting just a single step in the methodology, and adopting all five has been even more profound.

Getting the most out of this book will be based upon your situation and needs. Read it from cover to cover or dip into it. There is a logical sequence. If you know your strengths then leverage them and start there. I don't subscribe to the idea of expending all your energy to develop areas in which you need to grow; this is not the most productive use of your time.

Certainly, read a step that you don't feel as skilled in. You are not expected to have an incredible depth and breadth across all five steps. As a leader, you need to be self-aware and, therefore, clear on what your 'towering strengths' are and mitigate the risks in the 'growth areas' that you need to develop. A good strategy is to understand your strengths and weaknesses and then surround yourself with a person or people who are experienced or talented in the areas where you need to develop. This mitigates risk.

The steps to be followed are simple, but the implementation process may not be easy nor will changes be achieved overnight. Changing into a Leader of Substance will challenge you, but the investment will release you from the merry-go-round.

Drawing on a wealth of knowledge and experience, I share personal stories from time spent working in large corporate environments, and as a consultant. When you finish this book, I want you to feel a growing sense of excitement about the organisation, departments, or areas you can lead by being your best self.

Part 1

THE POWER OF TUNING IN

WHAT LEADERS LONG FOR

This book is based on qualitative research involving just over 150 senior leaders from a range of industries. When I set out to write it, I was confident that I knew the problems we all face. I'd faced them too; I was a senior leader in the corporate world for a long time. But I wanted to be sure. I wanted this book to be based on sound research. I selected participants from among my clients and balanced these with participants with whom I had never worked before. I approached them with a short survey of eight questions.

Perhaps one of the most astonishing results of my research was the completion rate: 100 percent. Despite the incredible time pressures they face, senior leaders want to share their problems and insights with people who might help them. They are always looking for solutions.

I asked participants about their dominant problems. Specifically, what are your top three problems? What stresses you out? If you find yourself worrying, what is it about? What are your top three problems?

Time away from operations to think about strategy

Leaders told me that even though they are in a senior role and they know that they should be spending a good chunk of their time working strategically, it isn't happening. Some of the specific comments on the problem of strategy versus operations are:

'The strategy keeps changing. So, how do I devise it and then translate it into operations, capability and behaviour?'

'Balancing the day-to-day operations whilst adding value to the key focus areas'.

'Establishing the agenda amidst other highly competing and revenue raising activities'.

I delved further and asked leaders to put a percentage on the proportion of their time spent working strategically or operationally. On average, it was around 10/90 split. They wanted it to be 20/80. My view, based on observing the best executives, is that the percentage should be more like 40/60.

The worry and sense of being out of control comes through strongly in their answers to my survey questions. Leaders feel anxious that they aren't contributing enough to the strategic direction of their companies or divisions. They feel frustrated by being bogged down in the operational, the tactical, and the minutia and not making the progress required is palpable.

But when they try to tip the balance, they encounter strong resistance. Some, who have made a conscious effort to change their way of being, report feeling guilty. They watch their peers and colleagues rushing around at a frantic pace. They worry about how their executive team will react. Will spending time on strategy be perceived as not putting in much of an effort?

Meaningful connections

The survey participants also felt that the sheer pace of their day restricted communication and connection. A consistent theme was a lack of open dialogue between the executives because they were 'resource poor'. By resource poor, leaders meant they lacked time, capability or capacity.

Q; What do you wish you had more of?
A: Open dialogue among my
executive leadership team.

Participants expressed their communication issues in a variety of ways: 'negativity'; a 'lack of unity'; needing 'an engagement boost'. However, it was expressed, that the lack of open dialogue meant the leaders sensed a lack of clarity about roles, performance, and the company's vision.

Leaders reported that they could not have the necessary conversations and healthy debate that allowed them to prioritise their company's focus for the next three years. And they understood that without this focus, there could not be a united strategy or alignment around a tactical plan for the immediate future.

They understood that the chance of their team delivering on the strategy is very limited when communication is poor. This meant their executives struggled to prioritise or make the right decisions. They lamented the lack of initiative and focus on implementation among their teams.

Q: What do you wish you had more of?
A: Doers. People to execute what is a
bigger strategy than resources and time
allow but the organisation needs.

Q: What do you wish you had more of?
A: Staff with commercial acumen
and initiative.

A clear sense of what matters most

The lack of communication led back to the cycle of busyness. Because their team did not know the key focus areas, they could not make informed decisions on the stuff that really mattered. They could not be a real 'dial-turner' for the business; they could not improve the company's performance. And this cascaded through every level within the organisation. Every decision landed back in the leader's lap.

WHY LEADERS STRUGGLE TO FIND SUBSTANCE

These problems impact the brain and its ability to function significantly. Leaders start to operate within limited assumptions. What would be possible if they changed these assumptions and replaced them with a more liberating one? Instead of feeling guilty about focusing on strategy, they might think, *my colleagues see me focusing on the things that matter and they are keen for me to share how I do that.* How would this shift their behaviour, and would it mean it was sustained?

Stakeholders demand more

In the corporate world, the CEO and the executive team have to satisfy and balance the increasing demands of stakeholders. Sometimes these demands seem in conflict and you have to make a decision as to what gets priority. This, at first, seems to be an impossible task. All stakeholders are important and all of them make demands that seem of the utmost importance to them. Some of the major stakeholders are your customers or clients, employees, shareholders, partners, suppliers, distributors, the wider community and, of course, the relevant government and regulatory authorities.

People are baffling

Yes, people are complex beings. We tend to categorise people to make it easier to know how to interact. I'm sure in your career you have completed at least one personality test, probably several. We often only see a small portion of a person's character at any one time. We know that there are multiple layers of complexity to all of us. I know that on the surface I come across as a real extrovert who loves talking to people. This is true. However, on several topics, I am also an extremely private person and it can take a while to really get to know me. We can't generalise human behaviour and personality. The fact is we are unique and want to be treated as individuals.

Technology won't stand still

Technology is progressing at an exponential rate. A prime example is the doubling of computer processing speed every 18 months, known as Moore's Law. If you consider the implications of such exponential growth in your organisation, the possibilities are mind blowing and not always intuitive. There is an exciting aspect of this for Leaders of Substance: we may achieve what we dare to imagine while we are leaders in our organisations, our communities and the world.

Honest feedback

It is hard to strike that elusive balance of positive accolades and criticism, especially as a leader. Most of you would have given or received a feedback sandwich or two. This is where you sandwich a criticism or negative comment between two positive ones. We are smart beings. When we are on the receiving end of a feedback sandwich, everything said before and after the criticism is negated as we wait for the punch.

Many leaders I meet are unskilled and dislike giving and receiving honest feedback. This is a huge problem for our organisations. The goal of giving and receiving honest feedback is to improve an individual's performance and, therefore, the businesses. For people to understand the feedback, we need to just say it and not try to sandwich or dilute it. A Leader of Substance works diligently on forming deep connections with their workplace relationships, which takes time and effort. This provides a terrific basis on which to give and receive feedback whether it is positive or negative.

Rewards are skewed to short-term goals

There seems to be a lack of interest among senior executives to take a risk that may pay off in the long term because their professional rewards (such as bonuses) are skewed to short-term goals. In my experience, even long-term incentives are usually only a three-year duration. They are not devoting their focus to thinking what they should do now that will set them up 10 years into the future, when they most probably won't be the leader. As a result, leaders seem to be risk adverse and conservative in thinking about what is possible. Leaders of Substance want to have a long and lasting impact with the work they do, not only looking at what they are doing in their current organisation but more broadly in the world. They are strategic visionaries. They find a way to structure rewards that have a long-term vision in mind while providing short-term recognition and rewards along the way to keep celebrating success and keep the momentum.

THE MYTHS THAT HOLD US BACK

Woo-woo

There are many myths about relaxing the mind. People sometimes believe they need super human, Buddhist-monk-like or hippy qualities to relax. Or they think their minds are too busy to ever relax because their thoughts keep on coming. Relaxing the mind is not woo-woo, or pseudo-scientific bunkum; it is a way of gaining access to the subconscious mind and its creativity.

Of course, we can't empty our minds totally, and thoughts do still arise but we can learn to manage these and still gain some benefits from the process. The goal is to focus on the present moment as much as possible instead of planning your future or worrying about the past. There is nothing to achieve. There is no need to set yourself a goal to empty your mind—that would be setting most of us up for total failure. It is the nature of our mind to think.

Thinking is the answer

The natural tendency of the mind is to think. It is constantly thinking. In corporate life, we have overdeveloped thinking to a point where we quite often overthink. This overthinking can distract our attention and focus from what really matters. It can also make us anxious or stressed out. Most people, including leaders, have not spent enough time developing a filter to sort through which thoughts they want to hang onto and cultivate and which ones to discard. We flit from one thought to another and this takes a lot of energy and attention. Many of these thoughts are inconsequential and don't make a difference to us or our organisations. Leaders of Substance are in control. They choose their thoughts and are able to relax their mind. When we calm the mind, we can draw upon our intuition, which is a valuable internal resource based on experience.

Do, do, do

Many leaders feel overwhelmed by the enormity of what they need to achieve so they just feverishly start doing. They feel appeased by a sense of accomplishment. They start writing long to-do lists for themselves and others. Then they work their way through an endless list-ticking exercise so they feel like they are progressing and making headway. Meetings consume their time and their already long days expand to encroach on their personal lives (even more).

In reality, many of these tasks are operational ones; they do not use a leader's strategic capability. When this occurs—and I've seen it in many organisations—everyone starts to operate at a level below their actual role. Then, the challenge to step back up and 'out of the weeds' seems almost insurmountable.

THE FIVE QUALITIES FOUND IN EVERY LEADER OF SUBSTANCE

Leaders of Substance 'rewire' their brains

A Leader of Substance is 'in the zone': everything flows effortlessly, and they achieve exceptional results. This idea of 'flow' was first named by Mihály Csíkszentmihályi in 1975, although this concept has existed for hundreds, if not thousands of years, most notably in Eastern religions. It is when there is absolute congruency between your subconscious and conscious mind. Today, we understand more about the brain science when 'flow' happens. Let me talk you through gaining access to your subconscious by relaxing the brain first.

Recent research into the brain has shown that it is 'plastic', meaning it can develop new neural pathways. Until recently, neuroscientists thought our brain's pathways were fixed by the age of 25 years. In his book *The Brain that Changes Itself*, author Norman Doidge, describes many extraordinary examples of people who have overcome the impact of significant brain damage by 'rewiring' their brains. The term for our brain's ability to reconfigure itself is neuroplasticity.

In addition, further research demonstrates a profound connection between the conscious and subconscious mind. If we find, for some subconscious reason, we are not doing something we want to do and can do, it is now possible to shift our conscious limitations and assumptions, according to teacher, author and researcher, Nancy Kline.

Through coaching dozens of clients over the years, I've noticed when you relax your brain to a certain state, you can shift limiting assumptions, suggesting that it is the subconscious mind that creates the resistance.

There are several ways to encourage the brain to move into this relaxed state. And when you do—when your brain is relaxed—you will unlock the vast body of wisdom that is stored in the subconscious, which most of us have barely tapped into. Why is this untapped? Because most of us don't know how to quickly, simply and consistently relax the brain. In this book, I will share the secrets of how I have unlocked this incredible resource. This is a game changer as you are now working with both parts of the brain (not just the conscious mind).

As leaders, we all feel overwhelmed or out of control from time to time. Then seeds of doubt creep in to our minds. Sometimes, we push aside conscious doubt, and get on with what needs to get done. But what if we had a series of simple steps that allowed us to—on demand—squash that doubt and put it aside once and for all. When we access the subconscious, we tune into our authentic selves without the judgement and criticism of the over-thinking conscious brain. Simply put, we can get out of the way of ourselves.

Non-negotiable time to think

One of the best pieces of advice I received in my career was from my mentor and dear friend, Denis Bourke. Denis is an experienced executive and renowned for his design and facilitation of leadership development programs and his coaching results. To be strategic, he said, I must block out time to think. And I must make it a non-negotiable appointment with myself. Start each week by blocking out thinking time. Start small and build up: an hour a week, then an hour a day. Ultimately, allocate three hours a day to thinking and working on the business.

When I reflect, this seemingly small routine—which seems so simple but is very hard to do—is the key to all that I have achieved. These days, I spend at least two days a week on the business. Apply this rhythm and stick to it, and you will reap the rewards. At the start, my biggest problem was getting over the guilt. That is right. I worried about how it appeared to others when I say I am thinking, without producing anything, while my colleagues ran around, busy, busy, busy. Participants in my survey reported those same feelings of guilt.

Leaders of Substance are not 'busy'. They do not wear busyness as a badge of honour. Today, everyone is so busy. For me, busy now sounds like a negative. It means I am doing 'stuff' that doesn't necessarily matter, usually at such a frenetic pace that I am almost out of control.

To start changing my guilt around not being busy, I changed my language around this whole idea. If someone asks me how I am, I say 'full' instead of busy. Full has a completely different connotation. I have a full agenda, but it is intentional. I choose what I do. I am in the driver's seat about what activities I choose. As for what others think, I made a liberating discovery: most people are too caught up in their own busyness to notice what I am doing or not doing. So, I got over it and reaped the rewards. I encourage you to do the same.

Focus on what matters

Have you ever wondered how some leaders can focus their minds and produce copious amounts of tangible output? What I have observed is that they have absolute clarity on what they need to focus on. A friend of mine, Paul Brotherson from south-west Sydney, started with nothing and ended up building a global enterprise producing yearly revenues in excess of $138 million.

Paul has a great definition of focus: the force that makes us act, coupled with the removal of distraction. When he refers to 'the force', he wants to convey the idea that the alternative—not acting—is simply not an option. For Leaders of Substance, focus is a superpower that allows them to push past their limitations and achieve more than their conscious mind wants to think is possible.

Last year, I decided to trek the Inca Trail. This was a challenge that I had always wanted to do, and finally, five friends and I booked the trip to Cusco in Peru and organised the trail permit including the entry to Machu Picchu. To trek the Inca Trail takes four days and begins at an altitude of 2,850m above sea level. The second day is without a doubt the toughest with the highest altitude of 4,200m. In preparing for this 82-kilometre walk, I used Paul's definition of focus. It was not an option; to get there and not be physically fit enough to complete the trek, or to let my fears stop me from achieving this lifelong dream.

I was scared about two things: heights and being the slowest in our group of six. To overcome these fears, I set myself a series of goals to increase my chances of doing the trek well. I spoke to my coach. She suggested two courses of action. One was getting a specific fitness coach and, two was being prescriptive and realistic about what I could commit to. I followed her advice. To build up my fitness I started doing a Zumba class once a week. Zumba is a very energetic form of dancing and aerobic exercise to music. I also did a bush walk on the weekends. Over time, I built this up to the point where, each week, I did three Zumba classes, one three-hour street walk, and one bushwalk in rough terrain.

The first time I walked the ten-kilometre Manly-to-Spit bush walk in Sydney's northern beaches, I found it challenging. But I walked it so often in the six months before the trek that I was eventually able to run sections of it. I enjoyed finding my footing as I ran rather than being frightened of stumbling. To address my fear of heights, I chose specific activities such as climbing the Sydney Harbour Bridge with two friends.

It all paid off. When I finally got to do the trek, I was so familiar with my fears that I found them boring. I was over them. I had learnt to walk alongside them rather than let them control me. Sometimes, I would have a conversation with them. For example, I'd say: 'Thank you so much for trying to protect me and warn me of danger, but now you can move aside. My legs are strong, and I trust my feet. They will stop me from slipping and falling out from under me.' I still chat to my fears today whenever they arise.

Tune in to what works

Remove distractions. I switch off my phone and all notifications on my laptop, such as messages and calendar alarms and, of course, email. I make sure my family and dear friends know that I am going to be uncontactable for an amount of time. I ask them not to disturb me unless it is an emergency. In other words, I create an environment with no interruptions. Then I can do my best work. My output is of the highest quality, and I become consumed in what I am doing. I am 'in flow'.

What I find particularly useful is to use a timer. I block out time slots, usually one hour per session. I put a timer on and say to myself: 'Okay. Keep on going until that timer goes off. Then you can have a 10-minute break, get a drink, or a snack or a bathroom stop. I am always astonished in what I can achieve in an hour.

This is how I wrote this book. I wanted to write at least 30,000 words in six weeks. I went through my calendar and blocked out 30 one-hour slots. I know that I can pump out 1,000 words of draft content in an hour. If you want to be better than average, do a bit more than the average person is prepared to do. You will build energy and momentum forward.

To tune in fully, you need to totally disconnect and have plans in place in case of an emergency. Let me give you an example of an emergency. My mum passed away on my parents' 49th wedding anniversary on 6 June 2013. Less than eight weeks from my mum passing, my dad moved into a nursing home. He went from being a strapping, solid man who lived independently to suffering with the debilitating loss of memory caused by Alzheimer's Disease and severe frontal lobe damage to his brain.

His normal emotional responses didn't have the usual filters. The impact of his kind of brain damage can go in two directions: towards a very affectionate demeanour, or a very aggressive one. Thank God, my dad went to the very affectionate side. Even this has a confronting side. For example, he mistook the care of a newly qualified nurse as a sign she liked him. One night after she put him into bed, he leaned over to kiss her goodnight. She became nervous and understandably upset, and refused to work with him. The nursing home was short staffed. Before I knew it, they moved Dad to a mental institution. It was meant to be for a long weekend, but he was there for a few weeks. It was horrendous. After that experience, I needed to get away for a while.

I decided to go off the grid for five days and booked into a health retreat, Golden Door, in northern New South Wales' Hunter Valley. I told the people taking care of Dad that I was away and would only turn on my phone each night at 8pm for an hour. However, if there were an emergency, they could call the reception at Golder Door at any time, day or night. I found this hard to do. I felt so worried about Dad. But I knew I needed to unwind properly. I hadn't even had time to deal with the grief of my mum passing. I needed to turn my mind to Mum. And guess what? Nothing happened. There was no emergency. I called my dad each night at 8pm, and we had a good chat.

I share this story because it was a turning point for me. For two years before my mum died, I had kept my phone by my side and on full ringer because I wanted to be available to help her. Without thinking, I fell into the same routine with my dad. I made it my priority. As a result, my phone rang day and night. I became exhausted. I finally realised that I needed to recharge and take care of myself. I could not take care of my dad properly while I was exhausted and not functioning at normal levels. Even though I felt Dad's was a life-and-death situation, I realised I had to turn off and tune in.

And for most leaders in corporate Australia, although theirs is an important role, taking some time to think is not a life-and-death situation.

When I first stepped into a training role for the organisation that was then called the Retail Traders Association, I heard a great story about how to keep cool under pressure. A human resources director of a beauty products chain of stores once told me that everyone working there got stressed in the lead up to a big sales event. They tried to make sure that everything was perfect and in place before the front doors opened and the customers started to enter. There was a lot of work involved. This one time, a store manager saw that the staff had let the pressure get to them. Suddenly, he turned to them and calmly said. 'At the end of the day, remember we are only selling bars of soap. It really doesn't matter if it's perfect or not in the big scheme of things. No one will die if you have too much or too little stock out or it doesn't look as nice as you would like it to.'

We all want to do our best. But let's keep it in perspective.

On-demand light-bulb moments

This idea of on-demand, light-bulb moments is inspired by the author Tom Evans and a short visualisation from his book, *The Authority Guide to Practical Mindfulness*. He describes a light-bulb moment as a flash of inspiration where you can clearly see a whole image or picture. I always thought that light-bulb moments occurred only for the most talented and creative people. In reality, these moments are a lot more common than you may think. Tom Evans shows how you can tap into light-bulb moments whenever you want to. These flashes of 'enlightenment' or 'inspiration' come in to our minds, but also run through our 'three brains': the thinking brain, the gut brain and the heart brain. Let me summarise his explanation of what happens.

Firstly, an idea occurs in the pineal gland, which is located deep in the centre of the brain and was once referred to as the 'third eye'. This gland acts as a gate keeper. Be aware that if you are running internal chatter, this blocks your ability to access these inspirational moments. The idea gets grounded through your spinal column all the way down to your feet. This means that you feel a sense of connection to the earth that allows you to feel centred or balanced. Your mind checks whether this idea is safe for you and, more broadly, the world. The idea then flows back up to the gut brain. Your gut gives the idea a big tick or cross. The idea proceeds to the heart brain. The heart brain is an intricate network the same as those of the brain in the head. In fact, the heart sends more information to the brain than the other way around. If it receives the heart's seal of approval, the idea travels back to your thinking brain with confirmation that you are in love with the idea.

Now, the idea goes back up to the pineal gland and is filtered into the right side of the brain. The right brain 'sees' the whole image or picture and then passes the idea over to the left-brain. Here, we use our analytical mind do some final checking at more of a micro level. Then, it's back to the pineal gland. On occasions, the idea can move to the throat and the person then exclaims, 'Wow, this is a real aha moment.' Remarkably, this entire process occurs in a mere second.

Once you understand this process, you can cultivate these moments on demand. A daily 10-minute visualisation practice is ideal. Here's how:

Sit in a comfortable chair. I have my grandmother's old chair in my bedroom. It is slightly smaller and lower to the ground than my other chairs. When I sit in it my feet are firmly placed on the ground. I place my hands in my lap with the palms facing upwards. This assists to move into a meditative state. It encourages your mind to be more open and receptive to these ideas coming in. Decide what it is that you would like some inspiration on. Then start focusing on your breath until you feel that you have reached a relaxed state, both in your mind and your body. Let all the stress and tension melt away. Then start to visualise ideas coming into your mind and following the path exactly as described previously. With practice, any time you want to access a light-bulb moment, follow this short visualisation powered by your breath.

To make sure your ideas don't disappear from your mind, use a voice recorder app. As you think of an idea, say it aloud. Then listen back to them later and prioritise them. This way, you don't forget them. They are captured. Keep a list. One light bulb and you're on. There are numerous ways to tap into the power of the subconscious mind, and I use and have used meditation, hypnosis and visualisation. Each of these three ways allow you to relax the brain so that your brainwaves slow as the everyday distractions move to the distance.

Many people have asked me about hypnosis and what it is like to enter a trance-like state. There are of course many misconceptions about hypnotherapy due to the association with stage hypnosis. It is nothing like that at all. For me, it is very easy to describe; it is just like when you first wake up in the morning and you are still in that twilight dreaming state. You are aware of what is going on but are not disturbed or distracted by it. You may hear the dog coming up the stairs wanting his or her brekky or the kids stirring from their sleep, but you continue to drift in that relaxed state for a bit longer; it's like when you hit the snooze on your alarm. (An important side note though if you were to hear the smoke detector go off or an alarm you react and deal with that emergency.)

As we go through our normal working day, our brainwaves are operating in the 'beta' pattern. Beta pattern is where you are fully awake and alert and sometimes in the emotional states of being stressed or anxious. When you relax the brain, you slow down the brainwaves to move through to alpha, and in a deep trance or meditative state, to theta. These slower brain wave patterns naturally relieve stress and allow us to access and influence our subconscious minds.

This state is where your capacity to think deeply and clearly will occur because you can access your intuitive or gut brain when stress and anxiety is moved to the side. Bill Bennett made a documentary to understand intuition called *PGS: Intuition is Your Personal Guidance System*. This is where you will intuitively know what the right choice is to make. Normally it is a sense, or a feeling and you need to trust these instincts as this wisdom is based on a vast amount of knowledge and experience gained over years in your life. Also, where those wonderful light-bulb moments will happen on demand. Bennett interviewed 75 people: research scientists, quantum physicists, psychiatrists and religious and spiritual authorities. This and other research clearly showed that you cannot move from your thinking brain into your intuitive or gut brain when stress or anxiety is present.

Our conscious brain talks to us through words, and in that beta state, our brain can be over-stimulated. The inner critic can go into overload especially for those of us who are perfectionists. The self-doubt, fears and emotions can really impact the quality of our thinking. The subconscious differs and prefers visual or auditory ways of communicating. Quite often I will see clear images, pictures or colours in this subconscious state.

Another way that you can access your subconscious is to tune in to your creative side as a form of self-expression—this could be through photography, cooking or, in my case, Zumba. Or do something that is sensation-based because it allows your mind to switch off quickly and concentrate on feeling. It could be a sauna or a massage.

As you practice accessing your subconscious mind daily, you will find break-through ideas and solutions to the challenges you are dealing with. Always remember that accessing it is simple, easy and quick and it is always available.

HOW TO BECOME A LEADER OF SUBSTANCE

A summary of the five steps

The five steps are:

1. **Clarity**
   Know where you are going and articulate how everyone contributes.

2. **Connection**
   Create an environment to enjoy the ride with the people around you.

3. **Capability**
   Skill up to realise your vision and get maximum results.

4. **Capacity**
   Balance organisational needs with the available resources. And look after yourself.

5. **Check in**
   Stay on top of progress with your people and the measurements.

A relaxed mind is a prerequisite for this journey

It's simple to relax

How did we manage to complicate relaxing so thoroughly? There is no right or wrong way, but here is a simple method. Go to a place that has no distractions (technology, people) where you won't be disturbed. Sit comfortably. Place your hands on your lap, palms up or place your right hand over your heart to feel more connected to your spirit. Let the legs and ankles naturally fall open. Close your eyes or relax your gaze.

Breath and awareness

You may want to record this short mediation practice and then play it to yourself.

Find a comfortable way of sitting (as above) upright and well-supported. Gently close your eyes or keep them downcast. Bring a sense of appreciation to yourself. Thank yourself for dedicating some precious time to this moment. Turn your attention inwards and pay attention to your body in this moment. Become aware of your body and the mind as you sit here. Notice the flow of feelings or thoughts from the day's events so far. Simply allow and acknowledge whatever is here. Give yourself time to arrive.

<Pause for several seconds>

When you are ready, become aware of the fact that you are breathing. Notice how you can tell that you are breathing; where do you feel it in the body? You may feel the sensations of the breath passing through your nostrils: a slight coolness or tingling in your nose on the in-breath and the warmer air leaving the nostrils on the out-breath. Or you may become aware of the rise and fall of your chest as you breathe. Feel the belly expanding with each in breath. Just notice where the sensations of breathing are the strongest for you and allow your attention to rest there.

<Pause for several seconds>

If your mind is wandering away from your breath, acknowledge where it went, and simply bring it back to the breath. Let your attention rest with the flow of the breath. Let your breath come and go in its own rhythm. No need to force or control it in any way.

<Pause for several seconds>

Feel the sensations of each breath as best you can. Not looking for anything, simply notice what arises in each moment.

<Pause for several seconds>

Allow the mind to settle into the experience of breath. Experience the sensations as the body takes in air and lets it go.

<Pause for several seconds>

Notice your tendency to want to control the breath, to make it different to what it is.

<Pause for several seconds>

Follow each breath as best you can. Follow each inhalation all the way up to the small pause as the breath turns and becomes the exhalation and then follow all the moments of the exhalation. Notice the gap in between the exhalation and the inhalation.

<Long pause>

Allow the breath to be as it is, deep or shallow, long or short, constricted or smooth. See if it's possible to receive the breath, exactly as it is, without needing to change or alter anything. Simply accept what is.

<Pause for several seconds>

Now take a few fuller breaths, down into the belly. Become aware of your body in the chair, your feet on the floor. And when you are ready, gently open your eyes.

How was that? How do you feel? It lasted just a few minutes. It doesn't take much time to bring about a state of calmness and relaxation, does it?

Instantly calmer

Need to calm your mind in an instant? Take six long, deep, slow breaths. At first, try to take the same amount of time with both the in- and out-breath. Pause at the top of the inhalation and the bottom of the exhalation and notice if there is a difference in temperature between the in- and out-breath. The more you focus on the breath, the more you'll relax the brain. After you have practiced for a week or two, try to let the outbreath be longer. (It might take a while to master. That's perfectly okay.)

There's an app

Heaps of apps will help you relax and grow calmer. I love one called 'Insight Timer', which is free, and has over 3,400,000 users for over 8,000 guided meditations and hypnotherapy, music, and talks from many different teachers.

Consistency creates calm

When you relax and mediate consistently, even for a few minutes a day, you will notice how much calmer you become.

When I worked at the National Rugby League, I managed just three minutes before I left the house to drive to work. Some days that three minutes seemed impossible; a crisis demanded that I get to work quickly. Then instead, I would make the time at lunch. When you feel ready, increase your time to five, ten or 15 minutes. You'll notice the benefits.

Relaxation and meditation are the best tools in your toolkit. No equipment needed; you can do it anywhere, even if it's only taking a few full breaths as you sit in the car at the traffic lights or while waiting for your kids after school or sport. Make this a regular habit.

Moving meditation

The years I continue to spend studying martial arts, means I find it easier to go into a meditative state through movement. I often start the day with a series of five or ten movements that I don't have to think about and can just focus on my breath.

My first experience with my own subconscious state was in a guided hypnotic trance with my amazing dad. I was almost 16 years old and about to be tested for my black belt grading in Zen Do Kai, which is a freestyle form of karate. I got anxious and nervous before a grading, despite training consistently and doing the preparation. This meant that on grading day, I never performed at my best. I wanted this to be different. Mum and Dad were coming; I wanted them to burst with pride.

Dad guided me through. I remember the tears of joy that rolled down my face as I visualised the master instructor Gary MacRae (he was the founder of the Golden Knights club I belonged to) presenting me with my black belt, my certificate and grading sheet. I visualised the weeks ahead and felt the great sense of personal achievement that I could share with my family and friends.

Dad guided me through this several times. On grading day, these pictures, feelings and emotions came to mind, and I got my black belt. Not only that, but I achieved my ambitious goal of attaining this within two years, when on average it takes students five years (if they train twice a week).

At this moment, my thirst for accessing my subconscious and my whole brain began. I am so grateful my dad helped me overcome my fears. He also taught me self-hypnosis so that I could access my subconscious whenever I wanted with transformational results.

Mind training for failure

Hey, you know what? Even our best preparation doesn't always work. Failure sucks, let's be clear about that, but it is going to happen. Stuff goes wrong all the time. Most people don't prepare for this; they only prepare for the success. Leaders of Substance prepare mentally for this—it's called mind training. My friend Derek Leddie is an expert in this. He trained the South Sydney Rabbitohs who participate in the National Rugby League (who went on, by the way, to win the premiership in 2014 after 43 years). Train your mind like you do the other muscles in your body.

I suggest you read Derek's book that he co-authored with Amon Woulfe *Missing in Action*, to find out more about mind-training. But here is a quick summary of one moment in their training. They asked the players, *what parts of the 80-minute game don't you like*. Bad referee calls—they hated them. They reported getting so frustrated, annoyed, and upset that it cost them the game at times.

They asked what players did to prepare for bad calls. The short answer? Nothing. They spent hours training on ball-kicking techniques, but not a second on things that didn't go to plan. So, they were then asked, *what happens when there is a bad call?*

What tends to go wrong in your day-to-day work life? How can you mentally prepare so you can respond calmly under such pressure?

Ok, so now let's move calmly forward with the five-step method.

The five-step method

There is an irony implicit in this book. If you want to become a Leader of Substance, you need to do these five steps. At first, this is going to look like Doing MORE and not what the title promises: Do LESS and Be More.

How can I justify such an apparent contradiction? Let me simply say that once you have taken these steps, you will see and experience the positive difference. You will change, your team will change, and your organisation will change. Purposeful and agile, not merely busy. Focused and supportive, not toxic. Moving towards your goals, not running around in circles.

Why the five-step method works

For each step, there is a purpose and an outcome. One builds towards the next, but each provides huge immediate benefits. Start anywhere. Do anything that moves you towards becoming a Leader of Substance. Set your sites on a single goal: to do less and be more.

Part 2

BECOME A LEADER OF LEADER OF SUBSTANCE

STEP ONE: CLARITY COMES FIRST

THE PURPOSE OF CLARITY

You'll notice that this step is bigger than all the others by a substantial amount. That's because clarity is the most important quality you can bring to leadership. The desire of every leader is to see their vision become reality. They can only do this if they have clarity and can translate this vision into a solid strategic and business plan. It is the foundation that every Leader of Substance lays before they act. Once they have clarity, they are adept at prioritising and can say 'no'. They can also make the right decisions quickly. Your clarity will inspire others and energise you. Clarity gives meaning to what and how people contribute. Everyone is aligned and going in the same direction. Be patient. Read it all. Every part is important.

HOW TO FOSTER CLARITY

Trends

As a leader, you must work strategically. Before you sit down to set plans and priorities (coming up later in this chapter), you must be abreast of the matters external to the organisation that will affect those decisions. Make the time to build a solid understanding of your particular industry's context, trends and business drivers, and then look beyond your industry. If you are in the quick-service food industry, understand what's going on in retail, hospitality and the service industry. The big trend now is customer experience. It is not sufficient to just understand fast food and what is happening in Australia. There are so many brilliant insights that you can gain if you look across industries, sectors and in other markets.

Make the time to regularly synthesise, analyse and provide insights into the internal trends that you are observing. Doing this allows you to anticipate important events in advance and plan the actions you need to take. One way to get this done is to join a peer support network. I do this work with my clients. Every six weeks, I facilitate groups of six to eight people who spend half a day together.

A personal and professional check-in

Here are some examples of how my groups conduct a stimulating and exciting peer network. Typically, we invite a Thought Leader to share their knowledge and experience on a relevant topic. Afterwards, we look at how we can apply this knowledge back to our workplaces. Each participant comes to the meeting with a current business challenge front of mind. They share their challenge, and its context, the solutions they have tried, and what is or isn't working. The other members offer suggestions based on their own knowledge and experience. In an environment of trust and deep mutual connection, all the participants share, challenge and learn from guest speakers and peers. Focussed and robust conversations ensure that they leave each session with useful insights, tactics and tools with which to build stronger strategies.

The trust and depth of relationship in these groups is, I find, incredible. I cherish seeing the group members catching up between meetings and providing valuable external perspectives to their peers using the skills they have learned in the safe environment of the group. Members are clear about the benefits of belonging to such a network. Here's what they tell me they love:

✓ tapping into a wealth of varied experiences and perspectives enhance their ability to design initiatives and get them done.

✓ carefully selected guest contributors, who share their innovative ideas and research, means they learn more about the hottest, highest priority topics.

✓ networking with other experienced professionals in a safe environment builds a genuine community of practice and this accelerates their development.

When you regularly commit to a professional and personal check-in, you learn to understand your area of expertise, clearly articulate it, and demonstrate how it adds value to the overarching corporate strategy. While you may think this is obvious to those around you, it is my experience that these linkages need to be understood by a much wider audience. Many leaders tell me they are surprised to find their executives, board and shareholders need insights clearly explained.

If you read an interesting article, summarise it into a few bullet points and share with the rest of the executive team; explain how you think this applies to your organisation and circumstance. Just forwarding the article does not add value (but does add to their To-Do list) or demonstrate your ability to think about the business as a whole. Stepping into this role as trend-spotter is a substantial part of being a Leader of Substance.

CUSTOMER CENTRIC

When I start working with a team of executives, one of the first questions I ask is, 'How much time do you spend with your customers?' By customers, I am not talking about 'internal customers'—the people within their organisation—I am talking about the customer or client who buys the products or services. Sadly, I am always staggered by how little time executives spend in this way.

Understanding your customers is central to developing clarity about your leadership role. One of my first roles in retail was a humble one: merchandising. I rearranged the window or floor displays of the merchandise in department stores and fashion houses. The feedback came instantly as to whether I had made a good or a bad decision with the display. And I will never forget the satisfaction and buzz of seeing the impact I could have on sales with this simple tactic.

As I moved from front-facing roles into buying or human resources, I realised it was even more important to stay close to the customer. When I worked in the United Kingdom for Disney Stores, the retail arm of Walt Disney's movie empire, there were 64 retail stores throughout the country. My team and I would schedule time in stores every week without fail. I spent, on average, a day a week in stores. Being on site meant I could help make the enterprise run more smoothly. I remember visiting a store that was experiencing problems with the delivery. Products were delivered to the back dock of the shopping centre. We introduced a new system that meant the deliveries came on a forklift directly through the front door to the selling floor. We rescheduled the daily delivery to an hour before the store opened for the day. This reduced so much double handling for employees and saved a lot of time. Without visiting the store, I could not have offered this insight.

When I joined the global fast food enterprise, McDonald's, I had one weakness that my peers did not: I'd never worked on the floor. One of this company's strengths is that most of its leaders had once worked in the stores. As part of my induction and orientation, I trained in all the different sections, from dining room to the kitchen to McCafé. I worked all the shifts. We regularly had competitions and every person was expected to take an active role. This experience proved invaluable and informed many of my leadership decisions.

By the time I joined the global event management company, Staging Connections, I knew what I needed to do. I joined the team to experience the arduous task of 'bumping in' and 'bumping out' events. I had to don the black outfits that the stagehands wore so they were barely noticed as they carried stage props on and off the stage, and in and out of events. I gained an enormous understanding of the conditions that staff faced in a business that ran 24 hours a day, seven days a week.

I'm going to admit to a frustration with executives who become subject matter experts in a discipline and lose sight of the customer. You cannot possibly offer leadership if you are not close to the customer? Recently, I worked with a human resources director who had won approval to implement a human capital management system. When the chief financial officer eventually agreed with his business case, it turned out to be at the detriment of the HR director's own staff. He had only thought about the efficiencies that the business would gain from having an online system rather than doing the work on excel spreadsheets. When the system was implemented, the HR director lost two of his own staff.

I asked this guy how often he spent with the company's customers, what challenges they faced, and in what ways could his business solve those problems for customers in a full and remarkable way? I think we both know the answer. He knew nothing about his customers. Instead, he was making his and his team's role redundant. He spoke about the business as if it were removed from him, separate to him and his team. I had to say, and with some frustration, 'This is where you are going wrong! *You* are the business!'

PRIORITISATION: WHAT'S A YES AND WHAT'S A NO?

No doubt your list of priorities for the next 12–18 months is a long one! The skill of prioritisation is determining what not to do and then what to do. Before you can plan (which I address in the next section), prioritise. I use a simple and powerful prioritisation matrix to assist with this process. I have seen many versions of this tool over the years, and I have adapted it. You will need to establish the two axes that suit your particular situation. In the example below, I have used value and complexity. By value, I mean the value that the priority will add to the organisation; and complexity is about the relative ease of implementation.

Prioritisation Matrix

	LOW → COMPLEXITY AXIS → HIGH	
HIGH	**QUICK WINS** (need a smattering)	**BIG STRATEGIC ITEMS** (most preferred)
LOW	**FINE TUNING** (incremental value)	**BACK BURNER** (least preferred)

VALUE AXIS

COMPLEXITY AXIS

Big strategic items

Big strategic items are your preferred options out of the four quadrants because these will add the highest value. This is where you must put most of your energy and focus.

Quick wins

Quick wins are important because they give you and your team a sense of achievement early, and that keeps the momentum going for the big strategic items. A sense of progress is a motivator and will keep everyone excited about the bigger goals that take time to be completed, normally over a 12- to 18-month period.

Fine tuning

These are normally the initiatives that you have previously completed. You have put them on a regular review schedule (normally annually) as part of continuous improvement. This is where you have the opportunity to make small adjustments to ensure they are achieving the desired outcome. Tackling these will move them far closer to that elusive one hundred percent accurate and relevant.

Back burner

Just one word of caution on back burner projects. While these are least preferred, consider including at least one of these. Choose an initiative that has featured on the list over the past couple of years because tackling it will prevent it becoming a more pressing issue in the future.

How to rank your ideas into the quadrant

The criteria that follows is one I developed to help you choose from the full range of initiatives:

1. What do we want to be known for in 20XX? This will tie you back into your group purpose or raison d'etre.

2. Is it aligned to the overall strategic goals (next three years)?

3. What is the complexity of completion? Including:

    - Implementation costs (operating and capital).

    - The opportunity cost of not doing it.

    - The level of complexity to implement and the risk factors. For example, technical failure probability of results being unachievable and rejection by stakeholders.

4. What value will it bring?

    - Is this the one thing that will have the biggest impact on reaching your strategic goals (a dial turner)?

    - Are they a 'must do'? If it wasn't completed, would that have a significant negative consequence, for example, affect risk management or regulatory requirements?

5. What is our confidence factor that we will be likely to achieve it? This is normally a gut feel that relies upon individual's rational assessment gained from past experience.

    - If it is 80 percent or above, then it is time to take action. Time is always the gold resource.

    - If between 50 and 80 percent of you think it is likely to be achieved, then you may need to do more work to bring up your confidence rating or decide to exclude it.

How to achieve clarity and consensus about priorities

✓ Ask each individual in the decision-making process to rank the initiatives in order based on the criteria above.

✓ On a whiteboard or flip chart list each initiative down the left-hand side so it is clearly visible to the group.

✓ For each initiative, ask each individual for their ranking and write them up.

✓ Tally up all the individual rankings, and then divide it by the number of people participating to establish the average rating per initiative. You will end up with a consolidated ranking with everyone's input into the order.

✓ Use the rankings to open a discussion. This gives people the opportunity to discuss their rationale and gain different perspectives.

✓ Agree on a set number of priorities. You do this step now rather than at the beginning as it will be reliant on the amount that you have and from which quadrant in the priority matrix they came from. For example, one big strategic initiative could be the equivalent in complexity to implement as six quick wins.

✓ Remember that no one makes the right decision every time; the key is to make more right decisions than wrong ones.

PLAN TO WIN

A strategic plan is a plan to win as we referred to it at McDonald's. Now that you have your priorities, develop the plan. This will cover what you want to do, how to get there, and the success measures. So, which of the many formats for putting together a strategic plan should you choose? The following two are the most powerful I have found.

Strategic plan example one

To identify what goes in your strategic plan, take the following steps. (It's always easier to have your page in a landscape orientation.) Identify the biggest issue you want to address. Now, identify the number one strategy that would solve this issue. Follow up by breaking this strategy down into the various actions. Take these actions and list down the tactics needed to achieve it. Lastly, look at who is accountable for each action, the time to achieve each action, and the success measures.

Once everyone agrees, then identify all of the tactics that will need to be completed in the next twelve to eighteen months. Duplicate all of this information on a separate page and this will be your business plan. Add in the detail for success measures. For each success measure, add in three columns: the target, the year-to-date figure and the year-to- date versus the actual target.

Measurement

Target: this is what you want to achieve.

Year-to-date figure: this is what you have achieved from the start to the reporting date.

Year-to-date versus the actual target: this is the difference between what you have achieved to date versus what you want to achieve.

Strategic plan example two (this is a two-page document)

Page one is an overview of the next three years.

First, write in one sentence, what you want the company to be known for in three years' time.

Now list the three strategic priorities you will focus on. Each of these is worded in a punchy way, almost like a tag line (five to nine words). After each of these priorities, outline the three initiatives that underpin them. Each initiative has a heading and then one- or two-sentence explanations.

Finally, some organisations like to add in a one-liner that acknowledges the key business-as-usual activities that must be completed in order for the plan to be realised. Here is an example.

Page one: Overview

<u>What we want to be known for in three years' time</u>

A vibrant, high-performing culture that is compliant with our policies so we retain the best people who put in the effort and want to stay.

<u>Our strategic priorities to achieve this goal</u>

1. **Attract** the best people for the best organisation.

2. **Retain** the best people who put in the effort and want to stay.

3. **Develop** the best people through experience, exposure and education.

The three initiatives that underpin them (for this example, I've just taken the second strategic priority)

Retain the best people who put in the effort and want to stay:

1. Reward and recognise

   Give back to the best people in a way unique to this organisation.

2. Talent pipeline

   We have the best people and they want to stay.

3. People talk

   People know what's going on. We communicate effectively and regularly.

Business as usual

Foundations: the policies, processes and systems are embedded.

Page two

The business plan is best presented in a simple five-column table with the following headings:

Strategic Priority/Initiative/Goals/Timing/Outcomes

Strategic Priority: Retain

Initiative: People talk

<u>Goals:</u> (Use the following pages to help you with formulating these goals effectively.)

1. Establish an internal communications plan and calendar of events for the year. Include staff briefings, chief executive officer teleconferences, monthly social activities, and special activities associated with the business division.

2. Establish a people and culture presence on the intranet that creates a one- stop-shop for team members to access information, links to online tools, and online tutorials.

3. Establish a people and culture committee to drive the culture agenda.

Timing

1. FY quarter two: October

2. FY quarter three: January

3. FY quarter two: November

Outcomes

1. Increase in the engagement scores in the categories of communication from 21% to 40% and leadership from 32% to 40% in 20XX.

2. Reduce manual administration and reduction in the number of queries received.

3. A functional committee established by 30 November.

Goals: New thinking on how to set them and achieve them

Goals turn your ideas into reality by making them tangible and measurable. Across every industry, sector and seniority level, leaders consistently find it hard to write goals. I know this because I often coach leaders in goal setting.

I understand their confusion. Research around effective goal setting has changed. Back in the day, we learned to write goals using the SMART principle: Specific, Measurable, Achievable, Realistic and Time-bound. No matter how we tried to apply this principle, most of us found it difficult to achieve what we set out to do. Why? In my opinion, it was because it was a checking mechanism, where once you had written your goal, you'd ask yourself the series of questions starting with is my goal specific, measurable etc.?

Ten years ago, I came across a different methodology invented by PeopleStreme called VQTQ. PeopleStreme provide integrated Human Resources software and I first partnered with them whilst working at McDonald's Australia. The acronym VQTQ stands for Verb, Quantity, Time and Quality. In my experience, clients find this method more reliable to turn the seemingly impossible into the tangible. Here's how it works.

Verb

Choose a verb—a 'doing' word—to start off your goal. For example: increase, decrease, create, design or implement. A word of caution: there are hard verbs and soft verbs. Use hard verbs. This can be contextual, but words such as maintain or sustain are soft verbs. Consider changing them to a hard verb, such as increase, which is stronger. Clearly describe the action you desire.

Quantity

There are a million ways to qualify goals. In sales, choose a dollar or percentage increase. But you can also choose metrics such as utilisation rates, customer satisfaction scores, and staff engagement scores.

Time

Your deadline could be annually or on a particular date, such as 31 March. It could also be a project or initiative milestone.

Quality

My absolute favourite part of this goal's four-part structure is quality. This is what keeps the perfect tension or balance in the equation. It keeps you honest. Here is how quality makes the difference.

Below is an example of a VQTQ goal without the quality component.

V	Q	T	Q
Increase	Sales by 65%	by the end of the financial year (EOFY)	

The problem is that a simple way to achieve this is to give your product or service away. Add in the quality component, which in this case is gross margin, and the goal looks very different.

V	Q	T	Q
Increase	Sales by 65%	by the EOFY	while maintaining a gross margin of 32%

This becomes so much harder to achieve. The words 'while maintaining' are a good way to start the quality aspect of your VQTQ goal. For example, while maintaining 'business as usual', or 'adherence to legislation, policy and procedure' or 'service level agreements'.

Let's look at some examples of quantity and quality.

Quantity	Quality
Sales	Gross margin
Efficiency	Effectiveness
Time	Safety
Cost	Service
Resources	Staff engagement

The quantity and quality component may be interchangeable and the position of them is determined by your primary focus. Put the most important aspect you want to achieve into the quantity column. This doesn't mean we sacrifice quality, it just reflects the priority of our role. Let's go back to our example to see how this works. For a Sales Director, the focus would be on sales and for the Finance Director it would be on gross margin.

For the Sales Director

V	Q	T	Q
Increase	Sales by 65%	by the EOFY	while maintaining a gross margin of 32%

For the Finance Director

V	Q	T	Q
Achieve	A gross margin of 32%	by the EOFY	while maintaining sales volumes

Here is an example that needed some refinement to ensure it was a tangible goal. In the table below, I have put in comments about the problems with the first draft.

V	Q	T	Q
Deliver	Personalised, integrated and outstanding service		While enhancing the student experience
A good verb	Three goals rather than one	No time frame	How can enhancing be measured?

How can we make this more measurable? Let's be more specific about outstanding service by calling it achieving a student satisfaction score of 95%. Let's measure 'enhancing the student experience' by response times.

Then we rewrite this:

V	Q	T	Q
Achieve	a student satisfaction score of 95%	by the end of the calendar year	while maintaining a response time of within 24 hours

In the strategy document (above), use this method to clearly articulate the key focus areas so it is crystal clear what the organisation wants to achieve. There must be no ambiguity.

I also suggest adding a weighting to each of the goals based on the importance of them being achieved. The amounts should and will vary in most cases. It is unlikely that you will have four goals that are all weighted twenty-five percent, although, of course, you may. The total must tally up to one hundred percent. I do not include any goal that you believe has a weighting of less than fifteen percent, as it will most likely be the first to go when the pressure starts to mount. The reality is that goals that are weighted much higher, like 60 percent, are always going to be your focus as these are the real dial turners. If you are asked to add in a new goal part way through the year, then you can have an objective conversation with your line manager (CEO or Chairman). Together, you can reassess the priorities and whether it is appropriate to replace a goal that is already in progress.

Measuring success

A rating scale is a useful measure of success if you set it up at the start. If you have a five-point rating scale, then determine what constitutes the measure for each number. I suggest that the goal you have written would be a 3/5 and would meet expectations.

It is crucial that you and your team agree to the success measures at the beginning of the performance period. Setting these measures upfront avoids awkward review conversations. Let's look at an example below.

V	Q	T	Q
Increase	Sales by 65%	by the EOFY	while maintaining a gross margin of 32%

The employee achieves an increase in sales by 67% and maintains the gross margin at 32%. You think, 'Great! That gets a 3/5 because it meets my expectations'. They think, 'Awesome! I get a 5/5 as I have increased it by two percent above what was expected.'

Note in this example below, how ranges assist with transparency of expectations; for example, a score of 4/5 falls between 66%–70%.

5 = Increase sales by 71% or higher by the EOFY while maintaining a 32% gross margin
4 = Increase sales by 66%–70% by the EOFY while maintaining a 32% gross margin
3 = Increase sales by 65% by the EOFY while maintaining a 32% gross margin
2 = Increase sales by 60–64% by the EOFY while maintaining a 32% gross margin
1 = Increase sales by 59% or less by the EOFY while maintaining a 32% gross margin

Once you have these at an organisational level, devise goals at a divisional, functional and departmental level. The manager sits down with each of their direct reports to see how each can contribute to these goals.

The overall result is an organisation that has absolute clarity in what they want to achieve, and each individual knows how they are contributing on a daily basis to achieving this. It is up to us as leaders to explain the connections and links. These can seem obvious to us because we deal with the strategy every day. For more junior staff this is not the case. Leaders of Substance don't fall back on the easy excuses, such as saying, 'Oh yes! We told them all this at the roadshow and the town halls (an organisation-wide meeting where executives update employees and invite questions) that we ran at the start of the year. And it's on the intranet.' They take the time to communicate (because they create that time).

I have never known an organisation to be told, in an engagement survey by their employees, that they believe that leadership 'over communicates'. No one says, 'Could the leaders just please stop; it's too much'. In fact, quite the opposite happens. Better communication is consistently in the top three areas of 'opportunity to address' in most organisations I have worked with.

Speak and sound strategic

Leaders of Substance also know how to speak clearly. They are able to prioritise and sequence their thoughts in a logical manner, challenge the status quo and get people talking about underlying assumptions.

They also structure their verbal and written communication in a way that helps their audience focus on their core message. I have a personal maxim that I live by: give the prize first. What I mean is this: instead of building up to your main point, share it first. Your main point is the prize. It is the reason your audience listens to you.

Most people lead up to the main point by talking about the background and the options before they talk about the prize. By the time they get to the prize, they have lost their audience. If you give them the prize first, you can elaborate on the solution. Most chairs and executives don't care about the details, however, because this is how you will achieve the outcome. That's your role, not theirs. This is also the case when writing a strategic plan, proposal or a reverse brief (a document you send to your client after you have taken the initial project brief). It includes your interpretation of the deliverables, scope, timeframes and investment).

Let them know, in a sentence or two, what they will get, and elaborate further down (so they can choose to read or not). This makes it easy for decision-makers. It also reduces time if you do not hit the mark.

CHANGE AND STRATEGY ARE CLOSELY LINKED

To embed your strategic goals into your organisation will involve a change. Leaders of Substance understand and use change models to achieve their strategy.

Cast your mind back to previous initiatives that you lead. Think about one that was hugely successful and write down the reasons why (do this before you read on). In my experience, the success factors fall into two groups: good planning and people leadership. Now, look back at your reasons and see if they can be clustered under these two headings.

Have you noticed that it doesn't matter whether people perceive the change you want to implement as being positive or negative? It is just as important to plan and consider the people components.

The Four-A Change Model

Before we look at leading others through change, let's take a moment to understand how to you can lead yourself through change.

Author, Bernard Desmidt, in his book *Inside-out Leadership* uses The Four-A Change Model to illustrate how change occurs. I have applied it when I have faced a challenging time with a colleague or peer. I identify my current thinking and behaviour and clarify what I need to change to successfully resolve the issue. And yes, in most situations resolution involved me changing my mindset and behaviour.

A – Awareness

Ask yourself, what is the gap between the current state and your desired state? This is the first step to awareness.

A – Adopt

This critical step is what makes the Four-A Change Model powerful. Change means you need to adopt a new mindset. To do that, consider what limiting assumptions you have made that might have contributed to the current situation. Now, ask yourself, what alternative assumptions could you replace these with? What new assumptions could move the situation forward in a positive way?

A – Adapt

How can you adapt to a new way of behaving? What is one thing you could *do differently* to resolve the situation?

A – Achieve

The last A is about identifying the desired outcomes that would benefit both you and the other person involved? If the matter was resolved, what would you be saying, doing, hearing and or feeling?

The ADKAR model of organisational change

Now that you have a strategy for managing personal change, you are ready to look at organisational change. The ADKAR model of organisational change is useful for organisation-wide initiatives. Jeff Hiatt, the founder of change management company, Prosci, created the ADKAR model. Using it, you can be best prepared to facilitate, drive and lead change. The acronym ADKAR stands for awareness, desire, knowledge, ability and reinforcement.

Here is the process that I use to apply the ADKAR model of organisational change. Give it a try.

A – Awareness

Get all members of your executive team and board to spend a few moment's writing down why they believe change is needed.

Now ask them to write their number one reason on a sticky note and put all the answers on the wall or whiteboard. This fosters 100 percent agreement on the reasons for change, which is essential for change to occur. Also, this summation of the rationale must be used in all change communication.

D – Desire

Now ask everyone to write down their estimate of the overall organisation's desire for change as a rating. Use a scale of 1–10 with one being very low and ten being extremely high. Average the scores. If the result is less than nine or ten, ask each person to explain the reason they have given this score. Fleshing out this section will also feed into the communication plan. Depending on the scale of the change initiative, you might also ask leaders to get their direct reports to provide a similar rating. Doing so provides you with a macro gauge of what is ahead.

Now for the deliverables: the good, the bad and the ugly. Ask your team to list them. Remember, even if the overall change is a positive one, it may lead to some negative expectations or outcomes. Whether those negatives are perception or reality, it is important to understand the full gamut.

When I helped lead a transformational change in a large insurance company, we started with a mapping exercise of the 50 most influential people in the organisation. We decided that we had to educate them and move them to being advocates as fast as we could. We needed to establish a baseline in how supportive they were with the change and then measure it again after we had completed the implementation phase. It is similar to the net promoter score (NPS: when you ask customers to rate how likely they are to recommend you), and the ratings fall into three distinct group-ings: promoters, passives and detractors. Promotors are your ambassadors. The passive people are the ones who you really need to engage with. Detractors are normally the most vocal. You know what their issues are and can address them. 'Passives' can be detractors, but they give you no idea what they are thinking. It is hard to target your communications in a way that engages them.

Interestingly, the number one influencer in this insurance organi-sation was the team leader of the switchboard. More than anyone, she interacted with the public, the insurance brokers and all other intermediaries, the staff, leaders, executives and board members. It was vital to ensure she was a promoter.

K – Knowledge

Knowledge in this context means the capability your key people need to create successful change. Find out where knowledge gaps exist so you can plan ways to minimise or remedy these. (Note: You will find a method of identifying those gaps outlined in *Step Three: Capability*). Hire in expertise, move talent up though the levels or horizontally from other parts of the business or build it. An option in building the capability is to get a mentor to work with key individual(s) so the knowledge is being transferred from the mentor to the mentee(s). In time, the capability will exist within the organisation and you will not need to rely on external expertise.

A – Ability

Ask your team to consider what support they need to make sure they are prepared and ready for the change.

R – Reinforcement

The final step is reinforcement. Think about all the factors you and your team need to embed and sustain the desired changes, so they simply become the new way of working. This step is one of the most neglected. Leaders spend a lot of time implementing change, launching it, and then forgetting this step (sometimes called launch-and-leave). People are just so relieved that it is done. Actually, this stage is when the real work begins.

The most effective way to reinforce change is to add success measures, rewards and recognition to your plan. Most organisations build in a big celebration as the initiative is launched, and then they are ready to start on something new. Rarely have I seen a leader set key performance indicators (KPIs) for six months, 12 months, two and three years after the launch. Leaders of Substance know that this is critical to reinforcing any change initiative.

Managing resistance

The SCARF model of motivation

If you anticipate resistance in the planning stage is it easier to manage it. You can use this understanding in crafting the key messages in the communication plan. People's natural response to the unknown (change) is to react defensively. This response is controlled by the amygdala in the brain. The amygdala is part of the limbic system. It is a physiological reaction that occurs in response to a perceived harmful event, attack, or threat. The amygdala has three answers to the fear: fight, flight or freeze.

In a work context, 'fight' means to resist it. This can be in language or actions. Flight means to run away, perhaps even leave the organisation. Freeze in this context is when people stop doing something. They feel paralysed by indecision. Sometimes, all it takes with this reaction is for you to be very clear, with the person, on the next small step to take. Then it doesn't feel so overwhelming. These defensive reactions to the unknown, occur whether the overall change is positive or negative. The emotional brain takes over, and rational thought just vanishes.

David Rock coined the term 'Neuroleadership' and is the director of the NeuroLeadership Institute. This is a global initiative operating in 24 countries bringing neuroscientists and leadership experts together to build a new science for leadership development. David wrote about the SCARF model in his book *Your Brain at Work*. The SCARF model is a collaboration and influence tool. Use this to identify how to decrease people's resistance. You will also increase the 'approach response', which is when the rational brain resumes normal function and sees the changes in a balanced way.

Rock identifies five main motivators. They are:

S – status   R – relatedness

C – certainty   F – fairness

A – autonomy

Let's take a look at each of these in more detail, and how they can help you to understand and anticipate resistance to change.

<u>Status</u>

Individuals who look at how change will affect their relative importance to other people. Here are some strategies to address the status motivator.

Increase 'approach'	Decrease 'resistance'
Provide opportunities to learn and grow.	Be less directive.
Recognise an individual's increase in performance and comment on it.	Provide the context for the change and why it is taking place.
Provide positive feedback.	Build collaboration.

Certainty

The state of feeling completely confident in a fact being true or an event taking place in the future.

Increase 'approach'	Decrease 'resistance'
Set clear objectives.	Involve others in the planning process.
Over communicate. If you don't have any news, say so. Commit to a regular meeting day and time and always provide an update. Give people the opportunity to ask questions in a group and one on one.	Set clear expectations.
Be specific about timeframes where you can. Give a confidence factor rating. Say, 'We are aiming for the end of the financial year and have 80 percent confidence that we will be able to achieve this.' This helps manage expectations.	Unpack complexity and break things down into manageable chunks.

Autonomy

The level of control that individuals have over the situation or choices available to them.

Increase 'approach'	Decrease 'resistance'
Encourage self-directed learning.	Provide options and alternatives.
Be flexible about how work is completed. I use a football analogy: Provide the 'goal posts', meaning clear boundaries about what is required. Let them use the whole playing field, meaning give them space to create success in their own way. Make few rules but have clear consequences if they are broken.	Allow them to be an individual contributor in a broader team.
Create policies that enable your team to do their best. The corporate world forms policies and procedures in two distinct ways. The first is all about mitigating risk and involves articulating every possible permeation and makes action almost impossible. The second is all about enabling action: a few critical policies that are a line (or at most a page) in length.	Encourage them to collaborate.

<u>Relatedness</u>

The sense of connection that people feel towards others in their department, function or organisation.

Increase 'approach'	Decrease 'resistance'
Set up 'buddy systems', in which more experienced staff pair with less experienced staff.	Increase collaboration. Do more than creating the physical spaces for collaboration. Train people in how to collaborate.
Provide coaching or mentoring.	Share relevant personal stories.
Foster friendship and remove competitive rewards. One of the highest predictors of feeling engaged in the workplace is whether people have a best buddy, friend or mate at work.	Encourage connection.

Fairness

An individual's perception of a fair exchange.

Increase 'approach'	Decrease 'resistance'
Invite people to volunteer for tasks and projects rather than mandating them. An organisation I worked with asked for volunteers to help me create and define the values. To our wonderment, over 30 percent of the workforce volunteered, with terrific representation from all areas and locations of the business.	Increase transparency and ask yourself: 'Does the risk of keeping this decision confidential outweigh the risk of making it transparent?'
Invite others to set guidelines, rules or limits and what the consequences will be if they are not adhered to.	Ensure consistency in messaging, regardless of who is conveying it or what level of the organisation or area it is coming from.
Remember that fairness is a perception, so it is very important to ensure that the optics are a true representation of what is happening. For example, I was in an organisation and they said all roles would be advertised internally before an appointment would be made. The only exception would be if a person had been identified as a ready-now successor. This was considered fair because they explained when the exception would occur and were transparent on these occasions.	Explain honestly why the change is needed. Don't give a standard generic reason.

The RASCI Model

I worked with a newly appointed CEO who found herself in difficulty quickly. She was at odds with her community of licensees about when and how they should get involved in decision making. We put a table together, using the RASCI model below. Gradually over the ensuing year, people's roles and responsibilities became much clearer.

The acronym RASCI stands for responsible, accountable, support, consult, and informed.

R = Responsible	Who is responsible for carrying out the entrusted task?
A = Accountable	Who is ultimately accountable?
S = Support	Who provides support?
C = Consult	Who can provide valuable advice or consultation?
I = Informed	Who should be informed about it or the decisions?

I developed an action plan for her with the following headings. I have added in an example next to each heading so that you have a better understanding on how RASCI can be applied.

✓ Who: This relates to the actual person or a group, for example, the licensee community.

✓ Role/impact: You choose which role from the RASCI model is appropriate for the situation and what impact it will have on the decision.

In this case it is C. Consult on which products are best suited for the various marketing events in the calendar year.

✓ Frequency: The frequency of communication between you and the group.

In this case, it is quarterly.

✓ Purpose: What is the purpose of the various parties to invest their time and energy.

For example, licensees will provide valuable advice on the geographical nuances of the regions they represent so that the promotional calendar can be tailored to their needs. This is far better for them than a blanket approach across the country. For the head of marketing, they will achieve a better sales outcome if they take this advice on board (bearing in mind they are ultimately responsible for the decision. The CEO is accountable.

✓ Stop/Start/Continue: In order for this to be successful for both parties ask them the question, what is the one thing that you could stop, start and continue doing? And then you do the same.

Stop coming to me on an ad hoc basis rather than on the agreed quarterly meetings.

Start sending the meeting pack two weeks prior to the meeting so I have sufficient time to prepare.

Continue to ask me for my advice and consider it when you are finalising the year's marketing calendar.

Once this is completed, you can use it as a basis for a discussion on how you can work together to get a mutually beneficial outcome.

Quality questions

Agenda questions

Leaders of Substance influence the agenda of the meetings they attend. The best agenda frames each point as a question. People attending will be clear on what the discussion will cover, and their brain will automatically do some pre-work on the topics.

Designing agenda questions is simple if you follow this three-step process. Topic. Outcome. Question. What topic do you want to talk about? What is your preferred outcome. What question could you ask the group to get the desired outcome? Let's use an example to bring this to life.

Topic

Customer experience.

Outcome

The best customer loyalty program in the Asia Pacific.

Question

In your experience, what is the most important factor to consider when designing a loyalty program?

When the agenda topic is framed by topic, for example, customer experience, no one can prepare their thoughts. When the agenda item is framed as a question, everyone will start thinking about how to contribute and come better prepared and willing to contribute.

Allocate time to agenda questions. Consider how long everyone would need to contribute an answer. Is it 30 seconds or two minutes? Set clear time expectations and use a timer.

My top ten questions

I have developed a bank of my top ten questions for implementing change. They cut through waffle and get results. They are very flexible, and you can modify them according to the situation or audience.

1. How does this initiative (or role) drive or support the strategy?

2. What are the expectations or deliverables?

3. Which behaviours measurably affect the key performance indicators? (You are looking for KPIs such as revenue, profit, engagement, customer satisfaction.)

4. What differentiates high performers from average performers?

5. What differentiates this being exceptional versus average in year one and year three?

6. What challenges will be faced from an external perspective, and from an internal one?

7. What could impact the outcome in the short and long term?

8. What are the specific capabilities which X* requires to deliver a) the current business plan and b) the future strategy?

(*X could be the board, c-suite, executive team, or department head depending on the person's level in the organisation.)

9. What are the early signs of success and failure?

10. What do people need to know, do, or be to ensure its success?

High gain questions

Have you ever been asked a question that makes you stop in your tracks? You may not have anticipated this question, and so are not prepared for it. You pause and reflect. Great consultants use this technique; the information both parties gain is of the highest value because the questions elicit new insights.

For example: In the last year, think about the top two insights that you gained, and how did you apply them?

ALL-IN VERSUS 'SILOS'? IT'S A NO-BRAINER

How many corporates still operate in silos? Given all the research about the downsides of these artificial barriers between different parts of an organisation, the answer should be zero. It's not. Insurance companies are a case in point. In my experience, silos have detrimental effects on both internal effectiveness and the customers' experience. I once worked with an insurance company with different practice areas or specialisations. These included construction and engineering, professional indemnity and marine. Each area had its own general manager, leadership team and a team of underwriters. Over time, we realised that many clients of one area were clients of another area as well, but we were not doing anything to make it easier for our client to deal with us as a company. A different individual looked after them in each of the silos. Of course, this was not intended to make it difficult for our clients. It's just that we didn't stop to put the customer first and look at their overall needs.

We decided to get the data on how much double handling we were doing across departments. Once we had assessed the problem, we set a new KPI in each of the general managers' plans: to spend 20 percent of their time working across the business functions, and report back on any increase in customer satisfaction. Giving the general managers KPIs, with clear directions on what was expected and the time commitment, gave them the incentive to shift their behaviour. If we had just asked them to stop operating independently in their silos and start working collaboratively, it wouldn't have made much of a difference.

In the first year, we set the bar fairly low. We wanted people across the departments to spend the time together and identify ways they could help the customer. In the second year, we asked for a tangible result: an increase in revenue. In the third year, the goal was an increase in our share of the market, compared to our major competitors. As we became easier for our customers to deal with, we became more actively involved in partnering and working collaboratively with them on their challenges. Soon, clients found our work more valuable.

If you want this kind of change, you have to show everyone involved 'the prize' first. In this case, there were benefits for the customers, the overall division, the departments and the individuals concerned. Clearly articulate your expectations, set your team a measurable goal and let them know what they could do to exceed your expectations. Measure the response (so you need to start with a baseline).

If you are finding that silos operate between areas, departments, divisions or even brands, set some joint goals that require departments to work in a united way to achieve a mutual benefit.

CULTURE

Dr Jason Fox is a best-selling author, motivational speaker and Thought Leader. He is known for his expertise in leadership, motivation design and the future of work.

His clients feature many Fortune 500 companies from around the world. In his book *The Game Changer*, Fox states that 'magic' happens in an organisation when three factors come together—motivation, behaviour and culture. He defines motivation as 'the driving force that compels people to invest effort into the behaviour required to achieve a goal'. This is where you see individuals put in discretionary effort. Behaviours are the tangible demonstration of the values. You embed values through rituals, artefacts and rules. When you have these factors embedded, you have a strong culture.

Start with motivation

Motivation is how you move things from an idea to reality. It's important because we must act. Therefore, we need to understand how to encourage action.

Let me give you an example from management legend. A soap company produced, distributed and sold beautifully boxed soaps in retail stores. The head office started getting feedback from its stores that a growing number of soap boxes arrived in store empty. The business hired a consultancy firm who, in turn, sent a number of engineers to the factory to work out what was causing this problem. More importantly, their brief was to stop it from happening.

The engineers spent a morning on the factory floor trying to come up with a solution. While they were scratching their heads, one of the guys who worked on the factory line found a solution. He had noticed what was going on: the factory line wasn't keeping up with filling the boxes. In his lunch break, he popped in at the local hardware store and bought a standing fan. He placed it next to himself on the line. Every time an empty box went past, the fan blew it off the line. If the box had soap in it, it was heavy enough to remain on the line.

The guy had a simple, cheap and effective solution. He could have kept quiet. Instead, he felt motivated to put in that discretionary effort. He saved the company tens of thousands of consultancy dollars.

Ever heard of the famous 80s band, U2? Back in 1987, they were touring America to promote their latest album, *The Joshua Tree*. They arrived in Tempe, Arizona, scheduled to play that night. Feelings were running hot in Arizona that night as the local governor had decided to abolish a public holiday that had honoured Martin Luther King Jr.

The band received an unexpected briefing from the Federal Bureau of Investigation (FBI). An informant had told the FBI that a gunman planned to shoot and kill the lead singer, Bono. The information was very specific about the exact moment the gunman planned to shoot. It was when Bono sang the chorus from the band's iconic song *Pride (In the Name of Love)*.

The FBI urged the band to cancel. It was a tense moment. The band, U2, had always used their music to express their political and religious views. They intended their tribute to King to help sway the governor to change his mind. Unanimously, they decided to proceed.

As they came to the last song of the night—*Pride*—Bono shut his eyes, afraid that this was the end. Opening his eyes on the last note, he saw his mate, bassist Adam Clayton, standing in front of him. Clayton had decided to take the bullets for Bono. Why had he risked his life?

Well, the members of this Irish band from Dublin had known one another since they were kids. They formed U2 at school in 1976. They had toured together for more than ten years. After some members went through tough times, the band made a promise to one another: to stand united and always have each other's backs.

Every time I tell this story, my eyes well up. What could have been the motivation to go ahead with the gig, the song and for Adam to shield Bono? Loyalty to one another and their fans. Also, commitment to a cause or purpose; they wanted to make a point that one day—regardless of people's colour, religion or any other difference—they may live harmoniously together.

Now we understand that motivation drives behaviour. Let's discuss values and the tangible demonstration of them through our behaviours.

Values

I am in awe of the very clear values that U2 have and live by. Reflecting on the story above, we can see the values demonstrated: togetherness, teamwork, trust.

How can we, as leaders, create even a fraction of this in our businesses? The actions of the band illustrate three fundamental principles about values that will guide us:

1. Values must be developed by the people they affect; they cannot be imposed. The band had pledged to have each other's back as a result of going through difficult times together. This was not an edict from management.

2. Values are a decision-making tool. The band's commitment to progressive politics guided their decision to play, and their commitment to each other helped the bassist step in front of the band's singer.

3. Values must be woven into every part of the business, including recruitment, training, performance management and even when employees leave. The values that inspired the band held firm in good times and bad.

My work with Disney Stores in the United Kingdom taught me a great deal about values, including how to weave them into every aspect of work. This company took values seriously. They were a daily reality, not just espoused, and I found that refreshing. We used the company values as decision-making criteria, a way of making and agreeing on what was the right thing to do.

I noticed a congruency between the brand values (what the customers experienced) and the internal ones (what the employees experienced). When putting together a series of recruitment days, for example, I admired the level of thought the recruitment team put into how they treated candidates. The company was running a big drive to fill the seasonal peak period near Christmas. Whether the potential candidate secured a role or not, their interaction with the brand further strengthened their positive view of it. We showed them how much we appreciated them coming to the assessment and selection days. We thought about how we could make their time with us a valuable experience and create a deeper connection by making it fun and rewarding. We wanted to create a lasting impression.

I saw the same care taken in every step of the employee time with Disney, including exiting the organisation. Whether their departure was voluntary or forced, people were treated with dignity and respect. This reminds me of an important lesson that a colleague of mine told me she learnt from her yoga teacher. Her teacher noticed that nearly all yoga injuries occur when people are exiting a pose. As leaders, most of us naturally pay attention to how our employees begin with our organisation or transition into new roles. But when it's time for them to leave, we don't spend as much time thinking about how they might leave us with dignity, respect and without any harm. Leaders of Substance know culture is defined by every part of an employee's experience of the company.

How Leaders of Substance apply values

Hire and retain

Screen for behaviours that align with the company's values during recruitment. Ask candidates specific questions on how they have demonstrated the values in the past.

Manage behaviour

Ensure that performance reviews incorporate values by focusing on how goals are achieved, the process and not just the outcome.

Reward

Recognise aligned behaviours on an ongoing basis.

Educate

Show your customers and stakeholders what you stand for.

Clear values will inject that elusive magic into your business—a positive corporate culture—every day. You can't see culture or touch it but you can feel it. That is how we know it exists. So how do you create it?

How to create, implement and embed your corporate values

Craveable Brands operate over 570 restaurants across three iconic chicken brands: Red Rooster, Oporto and Chicken Treat. They are widely recognised in each of the markets in which they operate. I partnered with one of my clients, Craveable Brands to create, implement and embed their values. This was the result of a collaborative and iterative process with input from employees, executives and shareholders. When you ask people to be a part of developing values, you'll be rewarded with a terrific buzz in the organisation. Being a part of developing a culture makes everyone feel proud to belong to it. I will share with you the process we followed.

<u>Questions that elicit values</u>

- ✓ What advice would you give somebody about how to act in order to succeed?

- ✓ What should they avoid doing?

- ✓ What does it take to get ahead and get promoted?

- ✓ What behaviours are rewarded here?

- ✓ What does it take to fit in?

Consolidate this feedback. Create a word cloud (Wordle.com can help). It is a powerful way to share the results.

Here is what we came up with and a brief sentence explaining the essence of each of them.

- ✓ *We win together*, centres on partnership and collaboration. It reinforces the need to work together to create best practice and evolve great ideas.

- ✓ *We make a difference*, reinforces a high-performance culture. It focuses on personal accountability and having a say in bringing about positive improvements.

✓ *We are open and honest* shows integrity and trust are at the core of this value. It reinforces that we recognise and celebrate success.

✓ *We are customer fanatics.* Craveable Brands exist as a support to the stores to assist them in delivering to the customers. The customer is at the centre of all efforts.

After we had created the values, we ran a series of workshops to determine how these could be demonstrated in action every day. We provided some examples of behaviours but not a long or exhaustive list.

For the value *We win together*, we said a desired behaviour was to grow and develop ourselves and our people. Another behavioural example for the value *We are open and honest* was to talk about issues and problems as it's safe to do so. We wanted all employees to understand the essence of each value and feel clear about what we expected from them in performing their role. However, we didn't want to be too prescriptive; you can never think of every example. We wanted people to express the values in their own unique way. With that done, we were ready to embed the values.

Embedding culture

If you unpack the concept of culture, it is embedded into an organisation by rituals, artefacts and rules.

Rituals

Rituals are a series of actions or behaviours that are performed with regularity in a prescribed way. A great ritual will reinforce behaviours in a way that feels genuine to the organisation and its people.

Here's my morning ritual. At exactly 5.30 am, my 12-year-old Border Collie, Manzi, paws the side of my bed. If I do not get up, my young Kelpie pup, Bose, joins in and they insist I get up. I stumble from under the covers and we walk down the stairs to the laundry and I feed them. While they are eating outside, I put the kettle on and make myself a giant cup of tea. I sit down and sip it. My morning ritual always starts with feeding the dogs and a huge cuppa.

What is your morning ritual? At work, it could be morning huddles where a team has a quick stand-up meeting of up to 15 minutes. In it, everyone shares what they achieved the day before, and their focus for that day. Or it could be making the time to say a genuine 'hi' to everyone in the team.

Turn your attention to a specific and widely used corporate ritual —performance reviews. Ideally, performance reviews are about conversations. As Leaders of Substance, our goal is to decrease the time that it takes between what a person does and when they receive the feedback on their efforts. Reviews become living, evolving online documents, not reports that are created and then forgotten. They capture the conversation so you don't need to rely on memory at the end of the year.

At Craveable Brands, we developed two types of reviews to embed performance reviews into their culture. A formal review twice a year, and another called 'sprint' reviews. Sprint reviews capture the ongoing progress of an employee reaching their goals (business and developmental) and demonstrating the values. It is a way of recording the conversations between a line manager and the employee along the way rather than just waiting to formal review time. There is an incredible amount of work and effort that occurs between setting the goals and when the outcome is reached. Leaders of Substance review performance regularly.

Artefacts

An artefact is an object that has been intentionally made or produced for a certain purpose. A great example of an artefact is, shoe company, *Zappos' Family Culture Book*. As the company grew bigger, it wondered how it could embed its culture to sustain it. Their answer was the 'culture book'. It's a collage of unedited submissions, from employees within the Zappos family, of companies that shares what the Zappos culture means to them.

A new version is created each year and it reflects the feelings, thoughts and opinions of the employees. Like a yearbook, the *Zappos Family Culture Book* is a snapshot of the year through everyone's eyes. It's a beautiful coffee-table book. If you go to the website address https://www.zapposinsights.com/culture-book, it explains what the culture book is, and you can view or download a PDF version or contact them if you are interested in creating a culture book for your organisation.

Rules

Rules are a set of explicit or understood regulations or principles governing conduct or procedure. Sometimes these are unspoken, and they are just as powerful in informing people what is and isn't acceptable within an organisation. Think about some rules that you have in place like your policies and procedures. Now think about some new one's that you could create and embed.

We sought input from employees (regardless of their level) for ways to bring the values to life. Within a series of 'Let's Talk Values' sessions that we ran, we had an activity called the Good Chook Challenge (this is just a fun name because what unifies the brands is they all sell chicken). Small groups had dedicated time to brainstorm a range of ideas. We applied one criteria: it had to be an idea that would not cost more than $500 to implement. Each group picked one of their ideas and pitched it back to the larger group in 90 seconds. Each session, we picked an overall winner. We created a system for staff to vote on all the winning ideas, and implemented the chosen idea.

Even if you feel under too much time pressure, or have a geographically dispersed or virtual team, you can adapt this idea. Ask individuals to submit one paragraph, a drawing or a one-minute video. Put a realistic timeframe for submissions such as two weeks.

Once announced, the overall winner completes the challenge in a specified timeframe (we gave them a month). They must spend all the money. They report back to the leadership team on what they were able to achieve with the money, time and effort. Then this needs to be shared widely within the organisation, a simple way is that the presentation can be videoed and uploaded onto the intranet site.

Since then, Craveable Brands have instigated two annual awards to recognise top performance, one called 'Game Changer' and the other 'Rising Star'. Everyone nominated joins what is referred to as 'Da Club'. The 10–15 nominees are tasked with how to embed the values at all levels of the organisation.

Here are some examples of ideas that the nominees of Da Club have come up with:

✓ Logos for each of the four values.

✓ A visual representation of food in the wording of the values, for example, a slice of pineapple appears as the letter O.

✓ Each of their four meeting rooms in head office are named after the values. The frosting on the glass of the meeting room has the logo that symbolises the value on it.

This example shows that you cannot stop working on values or forget about them. To bring the values to life in a meaningful, relevant and current way, you need to ensure that it is an iterative process that is regularly reviewed. As a guide, I would recommend every 12–18 months depending on where your organisation is in its maturity cycle.

STEP TWO: CONNECTION STARTS WITH YOU

CREATE A CONNECTED ENVIRONMENT

Leaders of Substance develop the skill of being 'present'; this creates better communication with others. By present, I mean that you aren't distracted and can give whomever you are with, your full attention. This isn't easy; you always have a lot on your mind. But it benefits you personally because those around you will appreciate the new, improved, calmer, more attentive person you will become.

Learning to be present is not an indulgence. A focus on the quality of your relationships is essential if you want to improve the experience your employees have at work. We are social beings; we want to feel a sense of connection and belonging. The quality of our relationships at work has a measurable impact on our sense of happiness and satisfaction.

The leaders in my survey lamented the amount of time they spend 'doing' stuff to get results. By 'doing' they meant the tangible actions that they were completing. They regretted not spending as much time as they wanted to on 'being'. The definition of being is the way in which someone acts or behaves, especially towards others. I am referring to how we treat one another. If we treat one another consistently well, we feel safe and it encourages us to act appropriately, and the desired results follow.

The three most effective ways to build connection are to foster the following qualities in your workplace: ease, equality and encouragement.

EASE

I define ease as offering relief from a sense of internal rush or urgency. This allows the brain's chemistry to be in place. Explicitly discouraging urgency will create an environment where everyone feels at ease. Surprisingly, we get more done, not less, in a calm environment. Have you ever worked with someone who is implacably calm? They radiate a sense of purpose and clarity, and often humour. I am not denying the chaos and busyness out there in the big wide world. More than ever, we juggle so many balls. But Leaders of Substance resist busyness and instead carve out the time and the space to think.

As a facilitator, I insist on creating this sense of ease in the sessions I run. For example, I always start and finish on time. I keep the time so that everyone knows that they don't need to worry about it. I create a calm environment and stay calm myself. I manage expectations upfront by explaining the structure and timing of the session or day. I enquire whether anyone has a commitment they need to honour, and we schedule these for the break times.

One of my clients is a creative agency. Whenever their creative department needed to put a pitch together, they grabbed the relevant team members and said, 'Right, we have 30 minutes to be creative and come up with some great ideas to take to the client.' For those people who thrive on pressure, this was exciting. For others, who need time to reflect and think things through, this was excruciating. So, the same 30 to 40 percent of people dominate the conversation at every meeting.

We changed this. Now they start with a briefing meeting with all team members. Then there is time for everyone to reflect, either individually or in small groups, so they can then contribute to the discussion in the larger group. The agency has found that getting everyone's input leads to a better outcome.

You can create a sense of ease in your organisation using the techniques of listening, providing information and sharing appreciation.

Generative listening is next level

The best way to cultivate quality relationships is to focus on listening. That is a big statement, isn't it? Let me explain in more detail. The 'listening' I am referring to is not listening in the normal sense; it is the next level of listening. Generative listening is referred to by Otto Scharmer, in his book, *Theory U; Leading from The Future as it Emerges*. He suggests that there are four types of listening, with the fourth coming from a future-possibility mindset (meaning they are imagining what is possible). This is generative listening.

Nancy Kline, in her book, *More Time to Think* adds to this idea. She talks about the idea of listening to others in a way that generates new ideas in the person doing the thinking (the speaker), which I believe is another aspect of generative thinking.

While this sounds simple, in reality it takes practice. Here's some steps to improve generative listening:

✓ Guarantee not to interrupt the person speaking.

✓ Look at them (but not in a creepy way).

✓ Avoid even minor distractions.

Guarantee not to interrupt the person speaking

Have you ever tried listening without interrupting? We think we do this most of the time so how hard could it be? Next time, guarantee the person who is speaking that you will not interrupt them, even if they talk constantly for several minutes. The speaker's brain is anticipating interruptions because that is what normally happens in a conversation. When we promise the speaker not to interrupt them, their brain starts to fire up. Rather than rehashing what they have thought or said before, it takes them to the cutting edge of their thinking. You give the other person's brain the opportunity to think independently.

Look at them (but not in a creepy way)

Hey, don't do a creepy stalker stare. I mean a relaxed gaze. Have you ever noticed that when people think, their eyes move all around the room, or they write or walk around the room? However, at some point they will stop and look at you. When they do this, and see that your eyes are still focused on them, you signal your attention. You demonstrate that you are fully present and engaged.

Avoid even minor distractions

Taking a sip of coffee or some notes is a distraction. Having your mobile on the desk will certainly be distracting, even if it doesn't go off (which it almost certainly will). Distractions tell the person talking that they are of secondary importance. Removing distractions shows them they really matter and what they are saying is the only thing you are interested in. It means you really are present and you will become more curious about and involved in what they have to say.

This kind of listening behaviour can feel quite clunky the first time you try it. Stick with it. I guarantee it is worth the effort. When you show another person they matter, and you are genuinely interested in what they have to say, the quality of your relationships improves dramatically. Can you imagine communicating all of this to another person without uttering a word. Generative listening has that power. It is the next level of listening, and allows the listener and the speaker the rare opportunity of 'being'.

Case Study: I owe my listening skills to my mum

I realised the power of generative listening on a visit to my mother in the nursing home where she lived in Adelaide. Sadly, my mum suffered from Alzheimer's Disease for the last ten years of her life, which meant her memory deteriorated severely. In the last two years, she lived in a nursing home as she could no longer walk, talk, shower or feed herself. I lived in Sydney at the time, and of course, I wanted to spend as much of the time as I could with her. Whenever I was in Adelaide, I'd spend the day with her.

The first time I visited, I'd been with her for about six hours when the nurse on duty came up to me. With genuine curiosity, she asked what I had been doing all that time when it was clearly a one-way conversation. 'I heard you talking and laughing and singing to music,' she said. 'I saw you dancing around. How do you do that when your mum is unable to respond?'

I hadn't really thought about this. I surprised myself as much as the nurse when I responded by saying, 'Oh, well she does talk. She talks with her eyes. When I'm telling a funny story, I know when she likes it. I play music that I remember was her favourite when I was growing up, and I can see her eyes dancing and lighting up. I certainly know when she is not impressed with something or doesn't like it—it is immediately obvious.'

Tears sprang into the nurse's eyes. This reaction moved me, and helped me to realise that the connection I had with my mum was because of the attention mum always gave to me, and had taught me to give to her. Undivided attention.

Information

Robust working relationships form when we provide people with the information they need when they need it. Let's take the example of a meeting. Is the person you have invited needed at this meeting, or would somebody else be more suitable? What is being discussed? What do participants need to do to come prepared? What is or are the questions? What decisions need to be made?

Here's what can go wrong when we don't share information with the right people at the right time. A local council asked a facilitator to run their CEO's performance review. At the facilitator's request, the CEO presented for 20 minutes, outlining his achievements over the past year and providing supporting evidence. He was then asked to leave the room while the council deliberated. On his way out, he gave the mayor a thick pile of documents. Just the one copy.

For the next two hours, I watched the mayor take that pile of papers and try to read it, understand it, do some high-level analysis, and share snippets of information with the other councillors. (The council had asked me to review the facilitation process.)

What shambles. Since none of the councillors had the information in advance, they could not look through it, read it, digest it, make meaning of it or ask any clarifying questions. For some reason, when the mayor got the documents, they were not immediately copied and distributed. The two hours the mayor spent reading them wasted everyone's time.

It seems obvious that the ideal solution was to reschedule the meeting, provide everyone with a copy of the evidence so they could spend the necessary time needed to rate the CEO in a way that did justice to this person. Instead, the group just picked a rating, citing time pressures as their reason for succumbing to this faulty process.

Pre-emptive information

Here is a powerful question to prevent this kind of craziness: 'What further information does everyone need to participate fully in this meeting or discussion?' And, here's another question that elicits essential information just before the meeting starts: 'Is there anything you would like to share with the rest of us that, in doing so, would allow you to be fully present and focussed?'

When I facilitate a meeting, I go around the room systematically, checking in with each individual and making eye contact as I ask the question. Quite often someone will say, 'Vanessa, I need to make an important call today at five o'clock' or 'I need to leave 15 minutes early as I am on child pick-up duty'. This frequently changes participants expectations of the meeting. For example, I may shorten the meeting so everyone finishes together.

Hidden information

Sometimes a Leader of Substance has to bring hidden information into the open. This means being sensitive to non-verbal clues, such as silence or defensive body language. Often this is because people are avoiding or pretending some information does not exist. Let me give an example. During a recent half-day management session, my client had asked to work through the company goals. One of these was about collaboration. The tension in the room about this goal was palpable. It's hard to explain exactly how I knew that some participants didn't agree with this goal.

I responded to the tension by asking the group about it: 'Can you share with me what is really going on here? I sense there is some tension around this goal for some of you, and I want to understand that more. Who believes that this goal is something we need to focus on?' Suddenly, the conversation opened up. I had to change tack and we worked through the discussion. Collaboration was removed as one of the major business goals for this organisation.

Appreciation

When people feel appreciated, their brains work differently. They think more clearly. Appreciation actually stimulates the mind. And research shows that, in successful relationships, the ratio of appreciation to criticism is five to one, according to the Gottman Institute. A magic formula. The Gottman Institute is the culmination of Dr. John and Dr. Julie Gottman's life work as researchers and clinical psychologists. It is the most extensive study ever done on marital stability and divorce prediction.

Appreciation means offering genuine acknowledgement of a person's admirable qualities. To make the biggest impact when expressing your appreciation, use the Three S Model: sincere, succinct and specific.

Sincere

Appreciation only works if you are sincere and honest. Almost everyone can detect an insincere compliment. Take the time to recognise the qualities you admire in someone before you share your appreciation.

Succinct

Don't waffle. Just say what you appreciate about someone. You don't have to say why, but you can.

Specific

You are 'nice' is a very general compliment. 'I appreciate the way you always say hello in the mornings' or 'Your attention to detail makes you easy to work with' are both succinct and specific.

Receiving appreciation

People tend to respond to a compliment by saying something appreciative back. But this actually deflects the appreciation. Leaders of Substance resist that natural urge and just say thank you. The words of appreciation then resonate and embed deeply into your psyche. It also communicates sincerity and appreciation because you will not trample on what had just been said or fill 'air time' with a quick response.

Using appreciation in a group

Start and end any group session with appreciation by asking a simple question: 'What is one aspect that you cherish or value in your work and are able to express each day?' In closing, I quite often ask the question 'What is one action or comment that has ignited your thinking today, no matter how big or small?' My business coach of four years, Kemi Nekvapil, asks me at the end of each session: 'Vanessa, what are you walking away with from this session that you didn't have beforehand?' It's a question that stimulates my sense of gratitude.

EQUALITY

Nancy Kline has a valuable definition of equality that will challenge any bias you may carry about status, background or gender. Treat each other as 'thinking peers'. What she means is that you work from the premise that everyone has the same ability to think, and is, therefore, equal. And paying equal attention and affording equal time to one another, taking turns, and ensuring everyone has a chance to voice their ideas.

When we give equal time to one another, no one dominates the conversation, and everyone feels equal. The thinking of your group will improve when everyone gets the same opportunity to contribute their knowledge and experience, regardless of power differences or hierarchy. So, keep to the agreed arrangements and time boundaries.

At a recent full-day senior management meeting, we started by stressing the need for equality. The chairman, managing director, general manager and chief financial officer planned to attend for the first hour and a half. The chairman, who had previously been the managing director, had a reputation for being domineering and intimidating. People tended to clam up around him. But we stuck to the format of giving everyone equal time.

Afterwards, the feedback was exciting. Everyone commented that the chairman, for once, did not take up all of the available time. Instead, people had a chance to get to know him. He was more accessible and part of the team—not separate to it—communicating a sense that they were all heading in the same direction. This mind-blowing moment of insight resulted in this organisation setting up quarterly sessions on the same basis.

By the way, this works just as well in my 'speed mentoring' sessions. In the time available, everyone has the chance to act as both mentor and mentee. Equality is the premise of these. It doesn't matter what level you are, whether you are from a corporate or are a solopreneur, or how many years of experience, knowledge, skill or ability you have. Instead, these sessions support the belief that we all have something unique to give and receive. This leads to a genuine two-way exchange.

Diversity

Diversity is a much used and abused term, so let me start by saying I refer to two aspects of diversity: thinking and identity. Studies show that diversity leads to richer thinking because when people's experience is diverse, it is represented in their thinking.

Diversity is personal for me. My father was English and my mother, Dutch. Mum came from aristocracy and Dad from a poor working-class family in the north of England. As unlikely as it sounds, their divergence served me well and provided my life with rich texture and appreciation.

Before I talk about the impact of diversity on thinking and behaviour, I'd like you to meet some of the characters from my past that illustrate the kind of diversity that makes a difference. Once in a lifetime, a leader finds themselves with the best team in the world. This happened for me when I became global general manager of an event management company.

We had people from all different backgrounds, ages and experiences. One was a 23-year-old Indian woman whose husband had secured a role in Sydney with Deutsche Bank. She had both an engineering degree and a Masters in Human Resources, and so was highly qualified and highly analytical. She had applied for various roles, was turned down and started to think no one would give her a chance. In our recruitment process, we asked her to put together a training module on customer service and present it back to a small group of people. She researched and delivered this task brilliantly. The selection panel had no doubt that she was our pick. Several years on, after two changes in organisations and several promotions, she is now a manager looking after remuneration and governance with one of the four big banks.

Another member of our team, a 25-year-old, whose Spanish family had come to Australia, was the first in his family to go to university. All of the men in his family worked in the mines in southern New South Wales. He did a traineeship and a Diploma in Human Resources at TAFE, and then completed a Bachelor of Commerce. His first job in our team was as the human resources coordinator. Within three years, he was the HR manager.

Another team member had worked with the company since he was 17. He had started off as a trainee technician, learning all about audio visual, lighting and sound. By the time he was 38 years old, he was leading the company's Asia Pacific departments of learning and development, and health, safety and the environment. Actually, stop press! He just became general manager of the company's operations in Asia, in particular the expansion into Thailand.

Luke was 52 years and had been a friend of mine for some 20 years. In addition to his background as a sculptor, a writer, and an animal activist, Luke has an outstanding wardrobe of Vivian Westwood designer clothes. He started his career in construction, working with the team building the iconic Anzac Bridge in Sydney. Anzac Bridge has significance because of its technical qualities; it is a world standard bridge in scale, aesthetics and design features. Initially, he took a contract role for 12 months with us, and stayed for over three years before following me to the National Rugby League. He leads health, safety and risk, with a particular focus on managing counter-terrorism tactics in our major sports.

You've met just a few of the team. As individuals, we taught each other to become the best versions of ourselves. Working closely with our clients, we did amazing work. None of us could have produced these outcomes, alone or in small groups. But as a collective, the solutions we developed made a difference not only to our clients but to the whole industry.

For example, we created a ground-breaking safety application. Using it, our technicians had access to information that showed them how to perform certain tasks safely, how to report problems and escalate risks on their phones. Most of our people worked in five-star hotels or venues. Typically, our technicians did not have access to a computer on site, but they did have a smart phone or tablet. The resulting improvement in safety lead to us receiving many accolades and the Australian Human Resources award for the best use of technology.

Here's another example of diversity's impact. A group of human resources leaders that meets every six weeks recently asked me to organise a series of sessions about creativity and business. Various guest speakers came to the sessions, including a film director, an artist, a writer and the founder of an internationally acclaimed Australian business. I was astonished to find that when the HR folk and creative artists got together, they birthed incredible ideas for one another. These came about by applying skills from different industries, different professions and different countries to the challenges that everyone faced. The meetings ignited a lot of energy.

ENCOURAGEMENT

Give courage to those who go to the cutting edge of ideas, and move beyond internal competition between individuals or divisions. That is what I mean by encouragement. This idea is closely linked to appreciation, but is distinct from it. With appreciation, you recognise existing talents. With encouragement, you are fostering new ones.

Expressing encouragement is less about yahooing, and more about body language and intonation. You encourage people with eye contact and focused attention (as we have mentioned earlier). Your genuine curiosity about what they may say next communicates encouragement. Ask simple questions to encourage more communication, only when you believe the person has said all that they want too. One of my favourites is, 'What else?' or 'Is there anything else that you haven't had the chance to say so far?'

Feelings

Leaders of Substance allow people time to express their emotions and then to resume rational thinking. Years ago, while studying to be a counsellor, a facilitator ran an exercise where she asked everyone to stand in a circle and take it in turns to share a personal story related to the theory we had just discussed. She searched for a soft ball, which, she explained, we would hold while we spoke and throw to the next person to indicate who was next. She couldn't find the ball and grabbed the closest object: a baby doll.

To demonstrate, she threw the doll to one of the women in the group. The woman went to her knees and sobbed uncontrollably. My natural reaction was to rush over and hug this woman, try to console her or at least hand her some tissues. Like most of my fellow students, I felt an overwhelming desire to supress her distress. What the facilitator did next surprised me. She asked us to just allow the woman some time to release her emotions.

It felt like ages, but was probably a couple of minutes. Soon the woman recovered and told us that doll triggered a memory of something horrific that occurred when she was a child. Her extreme reaction was as surprising for her as it was for us. She worked through it knowing that we were there for her. It was a profound moment of leadership for me.

Whenever I am with someone who becomes emotional (regardless of how that emotion is expressed—anger, hurt) I allow them time. I don't leave. I just stop and wait. Pretty soon, the emotion passes, and our relationship is deepened and strengthened by the experience. And, we can get back to the matter in hand with speed and trust.

Place

Leaders of Substance put effort and thought into creating the physical spaces in which they work with others. Why? Because the quality of the place tells people that they matter. I am not talking about expensive furniture and decorations (although a good fitout will have a great effect on any workplace). The small personal touches make an incredible difference. The key to success is to think about the individuals involved combined with what you are trying to achieve. Whether you are choosing an offsite or an office, this gives you great insight into finding the perfect place.

I have a client dedicated to creating outstanding brand experiences for their customers. They are a creative and quirky bunch who relishes out-of-the-box thinking. Asked to deliver a one-day session to the senior leaders, I booked an old terrace house in the old-money suburb of Woollahra, in Sydney. From the outside, you had no idea what you were about to step into. The architect who owned the terrace had transformed the inside delightfully. In the boardroom was a massive old farmhouse table with crystal decanters that hung upside down as light fittings. The back wall was full of wine. Breakout spaces included everything from a courtyard garden to an atrium filled with a gigantic skylight and underneath that, a pewter nine-foot pedestal topped with a stunning mass of green leaves that spilled over its sides. Old-fashioned silver serving dishes hung on the walls as decoration. The large kitchen was all commercial steel with a table that seated 20 people. We all gathered and stood around it to conclude the day. The team loved it so much that they decided to run their own end-of-year party for all of their staff there.

During that day, the team created a three-year strategic plan, and an implementation plan for the first 18 months, a remarkable achievement for a one-day session. In former off-sites, which they told me were held in an old hotel function room with no natural light, dirty white boards, and tea that was indistinguishable from the coffee, they fell short of their expected outcomes. In my experience, the place can make such an important and incredible difference.

Rathborne Lodge is opposite the Art Gallery of NSW and part of the Royal Botanical Gardens. I led a session in which we had the space to ourselves. Being surrounded by the beautiful gardens was excitingly. Even more so, the day was a perfect 28 degrees, and we sat on the lawns working in large and small groups. The day got off to a brilliant start when, in my opening remarks, I asked each participant to say one thing that they were grateful for that day. Most commented on the exquisite walk to the premises in the warm sun, and how it felt like an inner sanctum tucked away within the beauty of the garden.

Creating a sense of place isn't complicated. Simple gestures, such as offering a person a glass of water and bringing a plant or flowers to the office, makes a difference. When I worked in an insurance company, one of my colleagues brought in a bunch of coloured Gerberas every week. She put them in a blue glass vase. This small gesture expressed a lot about her intention to create a pleasant environment.

Many a meeting room or boardroom gives away the secrets of a company's culture just by the way the room is presented. Chairs left pulled out from the table or empty tea and coffee cups left behind tell you no one takes pride in themselves, and the organisation in which they work.

THE BENEFIT OF CONNECTION

Internal or external connections are a support network to turn to when you need them. When you have a big problem, these are the people you call.

We faced a media scrum most mornings when I worked at the National Rugby League, with over 30 dedicated journalists ready to stick a microphone in our face and ask us a tough question. Being put on the spot makes you intensely aware of all your successes and failures. In moments like these, it is an absolute asset to be surrounded by people you know, like and trust, or at least to have spoken to them for ten or 15 minutes before the scrum begins.

STEP THREE: CAPABILITY: BUILD YOUR TEAM

WHY FOCUS ON CAPABILITY?

Building a capable team around you will set you free. Of all the strategies we talk about in this book, this one will most likely impact on your time out to think strategically and become a Leader of Substance. A capable team, that is clear about your strategy and is strongly connected to you, will make every day enjoyable, purposeful and efficient.

Yet many leaders simply cross their fingers and hope that their recruitment team appoints the right people. Leaders of Substance focus on identifying the capabilities they need and making sure that they work towards them every day.

LET'S PLAY CARDS

With your strategic plan now in place, it is time to turn your attention to delivering on it. The first question is: what are the capability requirements that you need? It is often a confronting moment (even for Leaders of Substance) to determine the gap between the capability they need versus what they have. So, turn it into a game.

Setting up for the game

You need a set of 40 cards, each with a different capability on it. You can buy them or make them. If you want to buy a set, Korn Ferry's Leadership Architect™ sort cards are terrific. They use four 'factors': thought, results, people and self. Then they break down into 'clusters': groups of competencies. Finally, these break down to the specific competency. Here's an example: the factor is self. The cluster is being authentic. Then two specific competencies: courage and inspiring trust. (I've used these competencies in the following three figures.)

You can create your own set of cards by brainstorming all your requirements. I use the following categories to make up a success profile, by which I mean the critical components an organisation should possess in order to realise their strategic plan. The four categories are:

1. Skills: what can they do? For example, effectively communicate.

2. Personality attributes: what are they like? For example, resilient.

3. Experience: what have they done? For example, managed a geographically dispersed team.

4. Knowledge: what do they know? For example, the organisation's bespoke e-commerce platform.

Place each capability on a card with a one-line definition (if required).

How to play

Choose 15 of the capability cards you believe are critical, and without which, you would be unable to achieve the three-year strategic plan?

Once you have this pile of 15 cards, place them into three piles: *essential*, *necessary* and *useful*. I acknowledge that in an ideal world, all would be essential, but I am forcing you to prioritise. There is a catch: you must put the same number of cards in each pile. Forcing an even distribution makes you differentiate between the importance of the capabilities.

You now have an importance rating. Assign every card that is in the *essential* pile three points, two points for every card in the *necessary* pile, and one point each for the *useful* pile. Write down this number. It is used in a report at the end.

Now you need a performance rating. Complete another card sort. Take the same 15 cards and place an equal number of cards into the following three piles: *talented*, *skilled* and *growth*. Assign three points for *talented*, two for *skilled* and one for *growth*. Write the number down for the report.

Conduct these same two card sorts (importance and performance) with a variety of people based upon whose input is desired. For example, you could look at the four levels of decision makers in the organisation: executive, manager, team leader, and high-potential individual contributors.

Gathering more data

Now it is time to talk with each decision maker about the information you have gathered. Ask them to elaborate and provide specific examples of talented people with skills they have rated **essential**. Likewise, ask for examples for their other answers: what are some specific examples of people who need development to achieve **essential** or **necessary** skills?

Now ask what they believe is needed to dramatically lift performance in the organisation? What would be happening if everyone was **talented** in an **essential** skill? What opportunities would become possible, and what would be the outcomes?

Your final question is as follows: 'Is there any additional feedback you would like to give that you haven't had the chance to comment on so far?'

Reporting on the results

Executive summary

Put the quantitative information—overall importance rating versus the performance rating of the capabilities across the various raters—into a spider graph. Draw attention to the three capabilities that have the highest gap between importance versus performance.

Figure 1: Spider Graph example

IMPORTANCE Vs PERFORMANCE

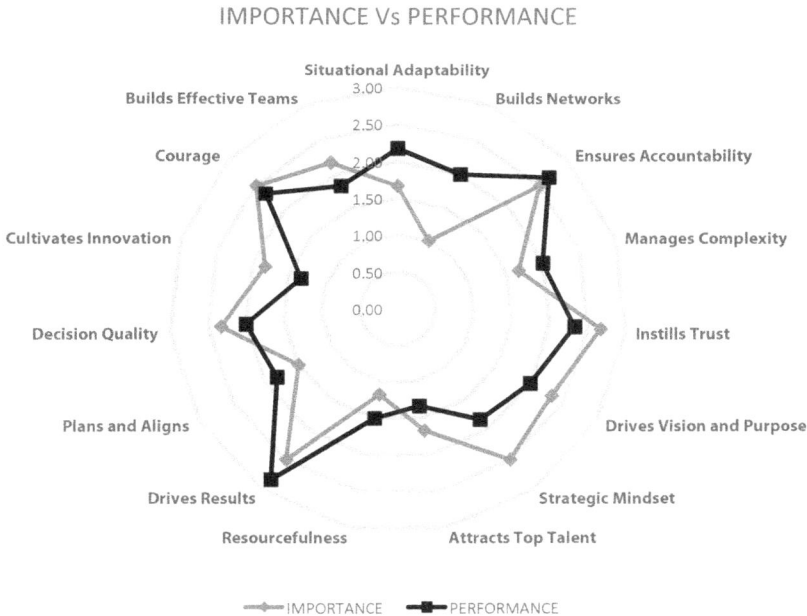

Source: Vanessa Porter

Follow with the qualitative information. Start with 'towering strengths': the three highest performance-rated capabilities. Write a paragraph on each strength, providing some examples from your discussions.

Next, describe 'growth areas': the three capabilities that have the highest gap between the importance and performance ratings.

Once again, add a paragraph or two on each capability, with examples.

Full report

Your full report has all the details and the action plan. Its sections are:

Quantitative results

✓ Importance rating of the 15 capabilities by rater.

✓ Performance rating of the capabilities by rater.

✓ Overall importance rating versus performance rating of all capabilities.

✓ A spider graph for each rater showing their importance rating versus performance rating by capability.

Qualitative results

✓ Expand your analysis of each towering strength to a full page. Then list the comments by groupings to give texture to the summary.

✓ Expand each growth area in the same way. Add suggestions to address the gaps and minimising the risk these gaps could cause.

Additional comments

✓ These are the comments in response to your request for additional feedback by rater or grouping.

This information can then be used to make decisions such as, *will you buy in certain expertise, grow it or outsource it?*

Figure 2: Prioritisation Wheel diagram

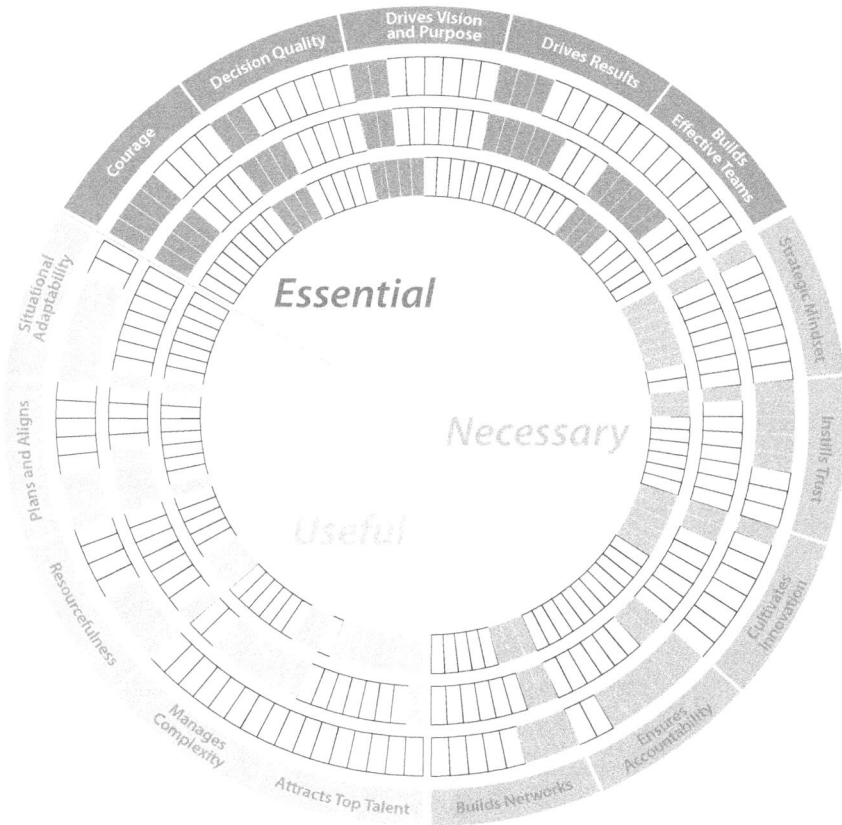

Source: Vanessa Porter

This wheel diagram quickly shows the results of the existing capability within an executive team. The CEO determined what are the **essential**, **necessary** and **useful** capabilities to ensure that they deliver on their three-year strategic plan. **Essential** are coloured the dark grey. These are courage, decision quality, drives vision and purpose, results, and builds effective teams.

Performance is plotted thus: the circle closest to the capability is **talented**, the second circle is **skilled** and the one in the middle is **growth**. The eight members of the executive team are represented by the little wedges in each circle. So, under the **essential** skill of courage, four executives perform at a **talented** level and four at a **skilled** level.

The table opposite can be used for succession planning purposes. My client listed 15 capabilities needed to deliver the strategic plan and scored them in terms of importance. Three is for those that are **essential** and shaded the darkest grey, two is for those that are **necessary** and shaded grey, and one is for **useful** and shaded in the palest grey.

Listing leaders on the left-hand side, the CEO ranked their performance against these capabilities: three is **talented**, two is **skilled** and one is a **growth** area. I have then shaded the boxes where there is a match between the importance of the capability and the performance of the leader at the desired level. A match between what is an **essential** capability and where the leader is rated as **talented**, is a dark grey colour. A match between **necessary** and **skilled** gives a grey, and lastly **useful** and a **growth** area is the palest grey. At a glance, you can then determine who is ready now to assume the role, and who may be ready in the future with some targeted development. Leader #1 in this case is the most preferred of all the leaders to take this role as the capability requirements and their performance are the closest match. They are **talented** in three of the **essential** capabilities and **skilled** in three of the **necessary** skills.

Figure 3: Executive Team as rated by the CEO

	Drives Vision and Purpose	Strategic Mindset	Attracts Top Talent	Cultivates Innovation	Courage	Instils Trust	Resourcefulness	Drives Results	Decision Quality	Builds Effective Teams	Situational Adaptability	Builds Networks	Ensures Accountability	Manages Complexity	Plans and Aligns
IMPORTANCE	3	3	3	3	3	2	2	2	2	2	1	1	1	1	1
PERFORMANCE															
Leader #1	3	3	1	3	2	1	2	3	2	2	1	2	3	1	1
Leader #2	2	1	1	2	2	3	3	2	1	1	3	1	3	2	3
Leader #3	1	1	1	1	2	2	3	2	2	2	3	3	3	1	3
Leader #4	1	1	2	1	3	1	1	3	3	2	2	3	3	2	2
Leader #5	1	1	1	1	3	3	3	2	3	1	3	2	2	2	2
Leader #6	2	1	1	2	2	3	3	2	1	1	3	1	3	2	3
Leader #7	1	2	1	1	3	3	1	2	1	2	3	3	3	2	2
Leader #8	3	1	1	1	3	3	1	3	2	2	3	1	2	2	2

Key

Importance	Performance	Rating
Essential	Talented	3
Necessary	Skilled	2
Useful	Growth	1

Source: Vanessa Porter

DEVELOPMENT GOALS

Development is a vital part of leadership. As a Leader of Substance, you need to choose where to spend your training budget and your development effort as a leader. You can see from the previous exercises that without a wise investment in training and development, you probably do not have all the skills you need to take your organisation from A to B.

Don't make development a feel-good exercise (as so many leaders do). Make it worth your investment of time and energy. Clearly articulate success measures before you spend any time or money on training and development. If you cannot tangibly measure the outcome, don't spend time on it. Measuring the impact keeps everyone motivated.

Develop your team fast. I have never spoken to a CEO who regretted moving too fast when it comes to development. Choose development goals that deliver you, your team, and your organisation the biggest return on investment. Whenever you receive a request for training, ask the person making the request for a few sentences that explain the payoff in each of these three areas before signing off.

After a team member crafts their development goals, ask them to describe in a few words what they will be feeling, thinking or saying to themselves when they have achieved it. Imagining these improvements helps people connect to their goals. Ask your report to come up with ten actions that will progress this goal. This gets them into the nitty gritty; their brains start working on how to achieve their goals. Now they can look at these actions, decide what is the top priority and what they need to do next.

Most people struggle with this. Getting them to workshop this with you gets them engaged and on to achieving that goal.

The development you provide can be a real differentiator as an employer. Talented employees look for companies with outstanding professional development, and they stick with them. I worked with a client who felt their competition was recruiting better people. The word among candidates was that other companies offered better professional development, and my client felt much the same.

In fact, this was wrong: my client did provide many development opportunities for employees at every level. The problem was they didn't make it known. They did not even *mention* development when recruiting. We started to quantify how much time employees, at every level, had with the managing director and executives of the organisation. It was staggering. The managing director facilitated quarterly innovation sessions. Everyone had access to coaching and mentoring, as well as quarterly lunch-and-learn sessions.

We added up the dollar value of this access, such as executive's hourly rates, time in spent in preparation for strategy sessions, coaching, and learning. It was a meaningful number as a percentage of their overall salaries.

The company started using this information in recruiting, expressing it as a real benefit of working for them. Their recruitment success jumped and so has their retention.

At McDonald's, we did a similar exercise. When each restaurant manager or corporate employee received their PAYG summary for the financial year, they would also get a summary of the development hours and dollars invested in them. Biannually, the corporation put on a week's training in an overseas location. In my first year, it was held in Berlin, Germany. Over 700 restaurant managers came from Australia and New Zealand. We asked them to complete Saville Consulting's Wave Styles assessment, which measured their motivations, preferences, growth areas and talents. That showed us the most useful areas of development. We offered a program of sessions to pick and mix. We bought in a range of internal and external experts to facilitate and evaluate these sessions. The company paid for their flights, accommodation, food, incidentals and all the training and facilitation. Imagine what a buzz it was for these people to be recognised for their work, and how it equipped them for the future.

WHY THE 70/20/10 PRINCIPLE WORKS

The 70/20/10 principle for learning and development is a formula that originated from the Centre for Creative Leadership. They were founded in 1970 and their solutions are steeped in extensive research and experience gained from around 2,000 organisations and 20,000 leaders annually in more than 160 countries.

When you are looking at developmental goals, try to divide the activities that will help employees achieve the goal as follows:

✓ 70% of the activities are experiential or on-the-job.

✓ 20% of the activities involve exposure to people who are subject matter experts, who act as a coach or mentor.

✓ 10% are educational activities such as formal courses or training.

Most people learn by doing, which is why the experiential activity is weighted with a whopping 70%. As the CEO of McDonald's registered training organisation, I had a budget of tens of millions of dollars each year to spend on learning and development. Mostly, we delivered this training in the restaurants. We called this 'shoulder-to-shoulder' training. People retain more of what they learn when they physically practice it, and then immediately apply it in the workplace.

The exposure model we used at McDonald's (about 20% of activities) involved first 'crew trainers' showing an individual how to do an activity, then coaching the individual to do it too. Finally, the individual does the activity on their own, and the 'crew trainer' observes and provides feedback until the person is competent to do it by themselves.

I'll share an example. I coached Luke, who at the time was the principle advisor on health, safety and the environment at the events management company I wrote about earlier. Luke had incredible technical expertise, but didn't have experience as a general manager, for example, developing strategy. He was keen to broaden his experience, so we set a three-year goal. The first year, in addition to his normal job, he shadowed me as I compiled the overall human resources plan. When we got to the health, safety and environment section, we discussed what the business needed and he wrote this part of the plan. The following year, we co-wrote the plan. The third year, we came up with the strategic goals together, and he wrote the whole plan.

Spend the final 10% of your learning and development on education. I am not suggesting there is no need for qualifications. But the evidence shows that workplace training delivers a greater return for employers than a generic training program, which is more suitable as a grounding or a refresher. Education doesn't show your employees how to apply what they learn to your particular organisation, department or situation. In-house training encouraging leaders to think carefully about how they develop their people rather than outsourcing to a supplier.

When you work on your personal development plan, choose a strength you want to leverage and a capability you need to develop. Two is sufficient. For example, judgment might be a strength and learning basic skills in Excel spreadsheets could be an area to develop.

MANAGING PERFORMANCE: HOW GOOD AM I REALLY?

Let me first define managing performance. I don't mean the old style punitive meaning, which is really a way of exiting employees from the organisation. I mean managing performance for the benefit of all. Everyone wants feedback on how they are tracking against expectations, what they are contributing and whether they are managing risks.

In my experience, the bottom third of performers will stay in the bottom, about half of those in the middle third can step up into the top quartile and the top third can give you up to 25 percent more than they may be giving you today. Some experts argue that you can't affect these numbers.

I disagree. As a Leader of Substance, you must engender an environment that encourages those in the middle to step up and the top third to give you that extra 25% of discretionary effort. Here's how. Ask yourself: how many of your employees fully understand your strategic plan and their individual contribution to it?

Robert Kaplan and David Norton from Harvard Business School (the American graduate business school of Harvard University) conducted research into that question in 2001. The results showed it was a shocking seven percent. In October 2005, they said it was an average of five percent. The Performance Management Institute of Australia in 2004, wanted to see how we faired locally when asked that same question, and to look at the variables across levels such as executives, managers and supervisors. Once again, the results were staggering. Even among executives, understanding stood at around 55 percent. For managers and supervisors, it fell to a mere 12 percent. Even when the executive defines the strategy, they only understand about half of the overall picture. They simply cannot cascade the information to the next level because they don't know half of it. Poor line managers, who are doing a great job of sharing all they know and understand, have only a tiny part of the overall plan.

Perhaps your percentages are higher. But ponder on the word 'fully' and then rate yourselves again. If your employees don't *fully* understand the big picture and how they contribute to it in their daily work, they won't be getting much job satisfaction. Let's face it. Most of us want to know we are making a meaningful impact, however small that is.

Executives excuse the ratings and think having the strategic plan on the intranet or doing a series of roadshows or town halls at the start of the year should suffice. No. What they must do is tie back everything they are doing, every action they take, back to the overall strategy, and clearly explain the linkages.

A Leader of Substance does this. Their genius is crafting their messages to be simple and easily understood. That is not an innate talent (usually). They test their messages with a range of individuals across different parts of the organisation and make sure they are understood. If employees at every level understand how they are contributing, you will see many positive results: engagement, retention, return on learning and development, and the overall performance of the business.

Look at profit per employee. This is a very simple calculation where you take the profit of the organisation and divide it by the number of employees that you have. It doesn't really matter if you are using gross or net profit as long as you are comparing like with like over the years so you can determine in which direction your trend line is going. With all the pressure in corporate Australia to do more with less, increase efficiencies and productivity, profit per employee is flat lining. And most executives don't know what that ratio is, even though labour is one of the highest costs in their business.

As a Leader of Substance, one of your main roles is to be a coach. I have worked with many great coaches both professionally and personally. They provide ongoing guidance to all individuals and the team as a whole. To use a football metaphor, great coaches don't deliver a one-off chat in the pre-season and then another after the grand final result. Does your coach see you every six months? No, it is usually fortnightly. Catch up with your reports on a regular basis and blend informal with formal.

The main reason employees leave an organisation is because of their direct manager. Everyone wants feedback and genuine appreciation when it is deserved. Your feedback has the biggest effect when you provide it as close to the timing of the event as possible. (Nowadays we are all used to getting instant feedback from social media.) People will appreciate your clarity and honesty if you just stick to one message per conversation—whether it is positive or negative.

Go into every discussion with curiosity and inquisitiveness. You will have some assumptions and maybe some facts, but you don't know the whole story yet. Ask open questions to find out the whole story before making any decisions. Make sure you respond, rather than react. If you feel upset, walk around the block or wait until you have calmed down before raising an issue. And focus on the issue not the person. Don't personalise feedback.

It's tempting, if you are strapped for time, to focus on your poor performers. This is unwise. In 2016, Gallup's ninth meta-analysis research further confirmed the well-known connection between employee engagement and key performance outcomes. They found that those in the top half on employee engagement nearly doubled their chances of reaching their goals compared to those in the bottom half. Couple that with the fact that high performers love feedback, whether good or bad. Make time to regularly schedule coaching sessions with your reports and make these a priority. Do not reschedule unless you absolutely have to. It is your role as a Leader of Substance to be accessible to your people in a real way.

STEP FOUR: CAPACITY IS A BALANCING ACT

WHY BUILD CAPACITY?

As a Leader of Substance, you must demonstrate to the board and executive team that investing in your initiatives will deliver the greatest return for your organisation. And, having done so, you must deliver on them.

In this chapter, we look at your capacity as a Leader of Substance to persuade stakeholders to your way of thinking, to stay away from busyness and focus on business, and to build and sustain your mental, emotional and physical stamina.

THAT'S A YES: WRITING A COMPELLING BUSINESS CASE

Your ability to write and present a compelling business case is fundamental to leadership. To lead, you need resources: time, money and people. To get them always involves persuading stakeholders. Every leader is competing for funds; most requests are either deferred or denied.

So why do the vast majority of business cases fail? In my experience, leaders do not talk about the return the organisation will get for its investment, nor do they back it up with sufficient data. On other occasions, the data is there but lost in waffle.

Make your case crystal clear, ideally on one page. What is the payback of your project and how long will it take? What is the cost to the business if you don't proceed? How does it align with the overall strategic plan? Provide supplementary evidence that shows your assumptions, data or research. Of course, sometimes there really are more pressing priorities, and you will miss out through no fault of your own.

The two most common mistakes

1. **Emphasise individual benefits rather than organisational ones**

   If you reduce turnover by three percent in one small department, it's impact across the entire organisation is much less. Your case won't stand.

2. **Assume it is fait accompli**

   Just because you have had conversations with key stakeholders, don't assume they are on board. Unless you can back it up with your business case, they will not support you when it comes to the crunch.

Whatever the size of your company, always make a business case. Even as a solopreneur, I prepare a business case before I invest. Some people rely on their years of experience or justify not preparing a business case based on the strength of their relationships.

The reality is it just makes good business sense. Clearly articulating in one page why you want the investment and what you expect to see as a result, ensures tangible and transparent decision making. And it covers your back.

Define the business problem succinctly and clearly. Paint a picture of the current situation and then show the future or desired state. Demonstrate the gap, how to get there and the resources required (cost, time and effort involved). Have hard numbers in your business case. What we think or hear from others is not good enough. Qualitative data that supports the numbers is great but is not sufficient on its own. No chief financial officer, chief investment officer, CEO or chair will approve spending without it (nor should they).

Example

Let's bring this to life. An organisation has 63 percent of its staff aligned to the business plan. The executive wants to increase this to 85 percent so that it can improve return to the shareholders. One way of doing this is to introduce a human-capital management system. This aligns goals from the overall strategy to each individual. This system requires a one-off expense, and a budget to embed it in the organisation totalling $315,000 over three years.

Estimated return on investment

The total of 630 employees equates to $50.4 million in payroll based on an average salary of $80,000. Since 63 percent are aligned to the plan, 37 percent are not aligned. Their efforts are not focused on the company's important goals. Assuming a complete waste of effort, energy and focus of 233 people at an average salary of $80,000, the total cost of this lack of alignment is $18,640,000. That's a big number.

Even if only 50 percent of their effort is wasted, the cost of **not** fixing this problem is over $9 million (50 percent of approximately $18.6 million). Now when you ask for $315,000 to invest in a human-capital management system, the pay-off is a no brainer. Even if it takes up to three years to get the alignment figure close to 100 percent, it is worth it.

Show your end goal and what you expect to achieve in annual increments. Put in a timeline and show what would happen or not happen if the initiative was delayed. Show tangible pain points, such as turnover rates or rising staff numbers that will worsen the losses. Often organisations can feel like The Titanic; they are slow to make decisions. As the iceberg was to The Titanic, these delays destroy what you are trying to achieve. Spell this out in black and white dollar terms.

The following is a simple way of putting together a good business case that I learned from PeopleStreme. The best way to work through it is by using an example, so let's do that. Create a three-column table with the headings: Issue, Evidence and Impact.

Issue	Evidence	Impact
Highly seasonal business with a lack of suitably qualified people during the peak periods	**Increase in labour costs during peak times**	**$1,152,300**
	Contractors need to be engaged during peak times	20 contractors for 15 weeks of the year averaging 36 hours a week on an average wage of $35 per hour = $378,000
	Make up pay for existing staff is through the roof	100 staff doing an extra 10 hours per week for 15 weeks a year is 15,000 hours at an average hourly rate of $29 is $435,000
	Three full-time recruiters spend 63% of their time on this alone	Recruiters earn $120,000 x 3 = $360,000, 63% of their time is $226,800
	Three operations managers spend 25% of their time on this issue	Operations managers are paid $150,000 x 3 = $450,000 and 25% = $112,500

Tally these numbers to express the business case in dollar terms: it is costing the business over $1.15 million. Now compare this to their other issues to see what we would like to prioritise as most pressing.

I take it one step further. I add a confidence factor to my dollar amount, for example, I may add that I have a confidence factor of 80 percent that all this is accurate. When you take this to the CFO, CEO or chair, they may debate the numbers, but they will get involved in the discussion. If you thought that the return on

investment on solving this issue was five times the initial investment, and they disagreed and said that it was four times, chances
are you will still get the funds.

MEETINGS

Capacity also encompasses the amount of resources you have
available. Time is a precious resource. I can't tell you how many
executives diaries I have seen where the majority of their time
is spent rushing from one meeting to the next. The standard
response to the question what have you got on today? is 'I'm in
back-to-back meetings all day'. Atlassian is an Australian enterprise software company with annual revenue of USD 619.9 million. They conducted their own research and found that most
people spend roughly one-third of their working week in meetings, and half of that time is considered inefficient. That's two
months per year spent in unproductive meetings. Yikes! Imagine
what that's costing your business. Why do we do this to ourselves, and other human beings—direct reports, indirect reports,
peers, colleagues?

As a Leader of Substance, stop going to meetings you don't need
to be at, and stop everyone else from doing the same. Take back
control. If you go to a meeting, build in time to prepare beforehand, time afterwards to digest, and do any follow up actions.
And allow a buffer between meetings to take a short break, get a
glass of water, or write down some key points before you need to
focus on the next thing.

Start questioning whether a meeting is the right forum for making
decisions. Meetings work when everyone contributes and comes

to a decision. If your meeting is a presentation or a briefing, can this be sent in an email or short video? If you don't want divergent perspectives, don't hold a meeting. If someone has called a meeting but isn't interested in your opinion, don't attend.

Work out your decision-making process at the beginning of the meeting. Is it a consensus, majority vote or something else altogether? That way, you manage expectations. Ensure the chair of your meeting actively participates and doesn't take on the responsibility of summarising. This leads to them assuming power, and controlling decisions. Summarising is a joint responsibility across all team members present. Ask a volunteer to write down the main decisions, actions and next steps. Or use a voice recorder app on your phone to get the main points. Transcribe or write it up later and circulate to all the relevant parties.

MATCH FIT

Do you have the energy to be a Leader of Substance? Many leaders tell me they are exhausted. What makes all the difference is knowing what matters to you. When things go bad, you have to know your meaning and purpose. Take time out to think about what makes the job sustainable for you. In my experience, family and friends always comes first for the majority of people. It is old school to lead your people to burnout, anxiety and depression. A Leader of Substance engenders an environment where people work in a state of flow and is clear on how this fits into their own reason or purpose in life. You help employees to find work and life integration.

Again, you might find my definition of work-life integration surprising: it means the resources you have internally that allow you to deal with the challenges you face. That definition comes from my friends at organisational psychology partnership, Eek and Sense, and I like it because it recognises that we are unique. We have a different combination of psychological, emotional, social and physical resources upon which we draw, and it is dynamic. Our work and life integration fluctuates depending on the events, challenges and experiences that we have encountered in our lives. We can't just compartmentalise what happens in life separately from what happens in work and vice versa. They are integrated and have an impact whether we like it or not.

Eek and Sense devised a Global Leadership Wellbeing Survey in six areas of work and life that have been shown to have the most impact. These areas are:

✓ Authentic relationships: with our family, friends, colleagues and the community.

✓ Meaning, purpose and direction: our overall sense of whether we are leading a good and full life.

✓ Resilience and equanimity: our inner strength and emotional evenness.

✓ Vitality and energy: our physical health, nutrition, exercise and sleep.

✓ Balance and boundaries: our success in balancing the various demands placed on us in all aspects of our life.

✓ Intellectual engagement and flow: our intellectual engagement and focus in the work that we do.

As a leader and a coach, I have found this survey a useful way to start a conversation or a series of chats to see where an individual is at. I've noticed that taking the time to understand a person from the beginning pays incredible dividends. Rather than waiting weeks, months or even years to uncover an area that is out of kilter, asking these questions early on means you will find out about issues before it is too late, and not as they are resigning. More importantly you can then access useful advice, resources and support that is targeted.

Plan with your significant others what professional success and failure look like. Set plans together. It can help to put your goals into categories such as:

- ✓ Personal development: what are the things you want to learn?

- ✓ Finance and or wealth: financial stress is the number one cause of relationship breakdown according to the marriage counselling service, Relationships Australia, in their *Issues and concerns for Australian relationships today survey,* conducted in 2011. Often, one person takes care of the money for a couple. Change that if you want to beat the odds.

- ✓ Relationships: who you want to spend time with and what you want to do with them?

- ✓ Health and fitness: what physical condition or shape do you aspire to?

- ✓ Career: what role or business would you like to be in?

✓ Community: what do you want to achieve in your local community, what kind of community do you want to live in?

✓ Happiness: what is one person, place or activity that brings you joy? This is not negotiable. When this thing happens, you can cope with most things.

When it comes to happiness, becoming aware of what matters to each individual in your team can be another simple way to build a great connection with them.

For me, happiness is hanging out with my dogs for at least an hour a day. One is 12 years and the other a young pup. For Manzi, the older one, we sit on the grass or I play hide and seek in the bushes. For Bose, the young Kelpie pup, he still needs his two-hour walks. I pat my dogs, talk to them, interact with them. No phones, no distractions. Just our precious time. It is very calming patting dogs who adore you as much as you adore them. As soon as they see you again, their tails go around 360 degrees (even though you may have just popped up the road for five minutes).

Learn how to minimise stress and make this a way of being. The mental health organisation, Beyond Blue, states on its website that, 'In Australia, it's estimated that 45 percent of people will experience a mental health condition in their lifetime. In any one year, around one million Australian adults have depression, and over two million have anxiety.' Given the amount of internal resources you need as a Leader of Substance today, you must be psychologically strong.

Energy is your most important asset; make sure you have energy left in the tank at the end of every day. That means you will respond appropriately when something comes up out of the blue.

Match day is every day!

STEP FIVE: CHECK IN ON PROGRESS

WHY CHECKING IN IS EASY FOR LEADERS OF SUBSTANCE

Once you take all the steps before this one, checking in on the progress of your people as they deliver your strategy will drop into place quite easily. In many ways, this is the goal of all the other steps. The check-in is your ultimate function as a leader. Stay focused on the strategy, stay out of the business, and focus your attention on ensuring your people can do the jobs you hire them for.

The first point in this chapter is about the general purpose and principles of checking in with your team. The rest of this chapter is about how to work with your human resources function to measure the performance of your entire company, and to monitor your profit per employee and the trend line.

CATCH-UPS

As a Leader of Substance, you need to keep people accountable and make sure they are clear about their role. How you structure catch-ups will depend on the number of your direct reports. If you have eight, a weekly catch-up would take up a full day each week, which is too much. Instead, I suggest you spend about ten to 15 minutes per person on catch-ups; this allows you to both stay on top of progress, identify problems early and still allocate sufficient time to thinking and strategy.

Prioritise by asking your report to rank their three most urgent or high-risk tasks. Then ask these three great questions (you can even set this up as a template):

✓ Are you on track or off track?

✓ What is stopping you?

✓ What decision do you need me to make?

As Leaders of Substance, removing obstacles is a big part of your role; about 50 percent of time, people are just held up by some obstacle. So, the second question is a powerful one. This will allow you to assist with the removal of them.

Working collaboratively is a fashion today, but it has a downside. People check in more and more with their manager to make sure they are on track, which really slows things down. In fact, this is not collaboration. It is a failure to think independently. As a Leader of Substance, empower your people with your clarity and connection and make sure they are capable. Discourage the need for constant reinforcement, which might just be a habit from their past way of working.

Give your team the 'right to play' and to make occasional mistakes. Think of it in terms of risk. Every year you can take one risk. If your people make a good bet, you'll see momentum really kick in. If they understand that it is ok to fail occasionally, mostly they will get it right. After all, your people are in the pulse of the business every day.

HOW TO MAKE HUMAN RESOURCES A PROFIT CENTRE

Leaders of Substance understand the full value of an HR team. A lot of their energy is spent making sure HR is effective, aligned with the company's strategy and measuring its performance. In doing so, you will shift HR from a cost centre to a profit-generating function. This encourages dynamic and creative HR practices, and an enthusiastic team that is understood and respected by the whole organisation.

The story goes that an HR director at a prestige car company presented to his board how HR had increased the company's profitability by four percent in the last 12 months. He broke it down so the board could see exactly how he calculated this. It was a mixture of cost savings that put dollars onto the bottom line, as well as how they actively contributed to new revenue streams. My point is that your HR function needs to clearly show how they are contributing.

Check-in regularly

Ask your HR leader to set up a dashboard with the categories listed below. This will bring together all the data sitting across your systems and in Excel spreadsheets to one central location that is easy to access and update. Finance and payroll will need to contribute to this data. You need monthly or quarterly reports on these metrics and their alignment with goals and budgets. Agree with the HR leader what you mean by a cost blow-out and ask them to draw any to your attention.

Key dashboard statistics

Your talent acquisition processes

The purpose for measuring this is to ensure that key and critical roles are being filled in a timely manner. If you have enough talent within your company, vacancies will be filled quickly. This is the ideal. Vacancies put greater pressure on your leadership, which is why you must measure the processes and improve them.

✓ What is the average number of days that the key and critical roles are open?

✓ What is the percentage of key and critical roles filled using people you identified in your talent or succession plans?

✓ What is the average cost to hire a new person?

Leadership 'bench strength'

Leaders of Substance measure bench strength to make sure they have a flow of qualified candidates to lead their organisation now and in the future. A systematic and transparent approach to these important measures creates constructive competition for future leadership roles. This fosters the feelings of equality and diversity that we talked about earlier; everyone has a chance to progress.

To measure your bench strength and start building it, start by considering each of the key and critical roles, and asking yourself:

1. What is the total number of candidates who are Ready Now (RN) and Ready in Future (RF) for that role?

2. Which key leadership roles only have one RN and one RF candidate?

3. Which key leadership roles have more than one RN and RF candidate?

4. How many are local (already living in the country you operate in)?

   Recruiting locally is usually easier. When I worked at Staging Connections, I noticed in the China office that developing local talent was often more effective than recruiting overseas. I had less difficulty dealing with the many differences in employment and taxation laws, visa requirements, language, and cultural norms (to name just a few).

Leadership performance

The reason for assessing this is to ensure that an individual's performance is being differentiated and that the action is being taken with lower performers.

✓ percentage of leaders who are rated: exceptional, significant, some improvement required.

✓ percentage of leaders rated as 'some improvement required' who have improvement plans in place.

Talent development

These measures are essential to ensure that your organisation is developing its talent and that the development is a shared responsibility between the individual, their manager and the organisation.

✓ percentage of key and critical positions whose incumbents have a written development plan that is discussed formally twice a year.

✓ average number of days per person spent on development.

Diversity and inclusion

It is critically important to recruit and retain people that reflect the customer or ideal customer base. I remember working for a large corporate in Australia, and at the time a lot of their marketing collateral featured images of young white Anglo-Saxons in their twenties to thirties. Yes, that fitted a percentage of the demographic but a small one. According to the Australian Bureau of Statistics census data 2016, we are one of the most culturally and linguistically diverse populations in the world.

Australians are born in close to 200 different countries, speak more than 300 languages in our homes, and adhere to more than 100 religions and over 300 different ancestries.

✓ What is the percentage of key and critical roles held by locals (in regional or country areas)?

✓ What is the percentage of key and critical roles that have one or more local replacement candidates identified or nominated?

✓ What is the percentage of key and critical roles filled by specific ethnic or minority groups?

✓ What is the percentage of positions held by men, women and X (indeterminate/intersex/unspecified) individuals?

Talent brand index

Your talent brand index is a measure of whether your brand is seen as a great place to work. You may choose to add other metrics, but the key to your brand index is to look at the result as a whole. A high result makes recruiting easier. If the result is low, the leaders need to formulate a plan to address the result.

Engagement

✓ How many people follow your business and engage in its social media content?

Risk mitigation

✓ How rife is industrial action?

✓ Do you have high forced terminations (versus voluntary)?

✓ Were there any terminations that resulted in claims being made to the business?

Employee recognition program

✓ Do you have a system?

✓ How many people use it by nominating others?

✓ What is the quality of the nominations in terms of what is being recognised?

Total full-time-equivalent staff

Numbers cross-referenced with the HR budget.

Turnover rates

The number of staff that leave as a percentage of the total staff numbers. Monthly, quarterly and annual figures will reveal trends that leaders must address.

Early attrition

Request reports on the numbers of recruits who leave in the first three months and the first 12 months. Ensure you have a plan in place if early attrition is high.

Remuneration

Compare to competitor's rates and set goals to meet or exceed. You want this to be in line with where you are positioning yourself in the marketplace.

Annual leave liability

This metric sits on the profit and loss statement as a liability, so your aim is to reduce the days and dollar value. A clear and connected culture encourages people to take their accrued annual leave because they feel safe and able to do so.

Engagement

Low engagement is often reflected in high personal leave or sick days. Ask your HR lead to provide you with strategies on how to address this.

<u>Safety</u>

Keep up to date on injury frequency rates and lost time as a result. Apart from the personal and professional impacts of injuries, these claims will increase your workers' compensation insurance bill. Ensure you and your leaders are building a safety conscious culture to make sure you see a decline in those metrics.

ALIGN HR TO THE BUSINESS STRATEGY

You have worked with your whole leadership team to establish the business issues or challenges (see steps one to four) and the desire outcome and key performance indicators. Ask all your executive team to agree upfront what they need from human resources.

For example, if the sales lead's KPI is to increase sales by $200 million, HR's KPI may be to deliver customised sales training across the entire sales workforce so there is a consistent approach to selling. As a leadership team, you agree what percentage the sales training will help in ensuring the increase is achieved? In this case, it could be 10 percent and then this needs to be measured and reported back on at regular intervals. Your executive must do this for each business priority set in the strategic plan.

CONCLUSION:
OWN IT

That is it! You now have a five-step process to become a Leader of Substance. What distinguishes those that step into this higher order leadership and those that don't? They OWN IT.

Leaders of Substance understand their contribution in the overall organisation. You now have a plan to build substance into your role. Your role is to engage everyone, from your reports to the front line, in the process of realising your organisation's strategy. To kick-start that process, you want to rapidly engage your team to support you in getting the steps done.

Engagement kick-start exercise

The following exercise is a sure-fire way to quickly build clarity, engagement and get the whole team working with you as soon as you walk in the door. Here's what you do.

Customer contact data comes first

✓ Gather your direct reports (up to 12 will work).

✓ Give them some sticky notes. Ask them to write down the big steps when your organisation interacts with its customers from the beginning to the end. These are also known as touchpoints. Ask them to write one per sticky note. Most should come up with six to 12 steps.

✓ Lay some butchers paper on the boardroom table.

✓ Ask for a volunteer to tell you what their first step was. Write it up. Go around the room writing down each person's first step. Repeat for all steps.

A surprisingly common result

Most people state the steps in the sales process. For example:

1. Demand generation

2. Qualifying

3. Brief taken

4. Needs analysis

5. Plan developed

6. Plan shared

7. Gain agreement to proceed

8. Project kick off

9. Implementation

10. Lessons learnt

A new perspective

✓ Now ask participants to write down how their role contributes to each step of the customer journey.

✓ Ask each person to add their sticky notes to the paper in the centre.

What emerges is clarity about the profound role that the support functions play in the customer experience.

For example, when step seven kicks in, and agreement to proceed has been gained, the organisation will need its staff to deliver on their promise. Perhaps HR needs to employ new staff to deliver the project and payroll must add them into the system, and pay them the right amount and on time. This process makes it remarkably clear that when the sales person is developing the plan in step five, they might contact HR and payroll so they can get prepared. Consider step two. Finance may need to get involved to see if the prospective client has a good credit rating.

When I do this exercise with clients, everyone is astonished at the various activities that go on at each step and the dependencies and inter-relatedness between the departments that make it all work together seamlessly. This is what provides a full and remarkable solution to the customer.

As a Leader of Substance, you will be surprised at how much better and deeper the understanding between your divisions will be. The exercise also fosters respect between divisions and highlights how they might work better together. Conclude the exercise by creating an infographic that captures all this information and share it with the participants. Ask your reports to do the exercise with their staff. Add the infographic to your induction process and keep it up to date. We don't need to know the minutia involved in each other's work, but we benefit from understanding the end-to-end process and each other's role in that.

THOSE WHO DO, AND THOSE WHO DON'T

Embarking on the path to become a Leader of Substance takes courage and determination, but I can guarantee that the effort will pay off. Adopt these behaviours to transform yourself, your people and your organisation. At times, the change will be challenging and you will sometimes face implicit or expressed resistance.

Although the five steps are clear and simple, they impact work patterns established over many years. Breaking habits and forging new ones takes tenacious dedication. I feel confident you are up for the challenge; after all, you have already started by picking up the book and reading this far.

The stories I have shared in my book and my explanation of the methodology are designed to help you reflect on your situation. You will find those reflections a springboard to new realisations.

I hope you feel inspired to step up and hold yourself accountable for creating a thriving environment—for you, your people and your organisations.

Like a marathon, the journey to become a Leader of Substance is hard to start. Resist the temptation to default to the simpler tasks that keep you caught up in the leadership merry-go-round of professional life. You now have a way to consistently and congruently become a Leader of Substance enabling you to create the time and space to manage the demands of your role differently and better.

You have learned how to stop scratching that 'operational itch' that keeps us so busy. Spending time on 'being' brings transformational results over time. You'll be amazed at how much more gets done across your organisation. Genuinely connecting to people, you will act pre-emptively and drive change.

In part one of this book, I introduced you to Tom Evans. I am going to refer to him again. He says in one of his mediations, 'Just for today, try something new'. Don't make the journey more complex than it needs to be. Resist feeling overwhelmed with the enormity of the task. Just concentrate on what you can do and incorporate today. If you continue with this daily focus and find a clear vision of your future, you will find a way to make it happen.

At the end of each day, ask yourself they five questions and set your intentions for the next day.

1. How did I help create clarity around the strategy from the chairman to a new starter?

2. Did I help create an environment where people have a deep connection with the work and one another today?

3. Did I learn more today about the capability we need now and in the future to realise the organisation's future strategy?

4. Did I balance the capacity requirements with available resources—budget, time and people?

5. Did I remain checked in and in tune with what matters most to me, my people and the organisation?

My best wishes on your journey

I welcome your reflections and feedback about this book. I have tested this methodology time and again, but there is no substitute for the lived experiences of those who have implemented my five steps. I'd love to hear how you go with them. I am as enthusiastic about learning from my readers and clients as I am about imparting my own knowledge. Growing is a two-way equal exchange because we all have something unique to give and receive. I look forward to connecting again soon. Until then, go and BE your best self.

Warmest wishes,

Vanessa

ABOUT THE AUTHOR

This book was written by award-winning senior executive Vanessa Porter. She has witnessed an increasing need to build diverse and empowered workforces that deliver on strategic goals. Her core belief is that we are all inherently equal. To this end she creates spaces where every individual knows that they matter. Her reputation has been built on providing strategic advice to businesses on people and culture challenges. Vanessa's solutions are high impact, deliver the right commercial returns and are sustainable. Her consultancy All Of You Pty Ltd works with some of the best brands.

If you would like to connect with Vanessa then please visit www.allofyou.co.

www.ingramcontent.com/pod-product-compliance
Lightning Source LLC
Chambersburg PA
CBHW030519210326
41597CB00013B/966